MASTERING CYBER HYGIENE: A PRACTICAL GUIDE FOR INDIVIDUALS

DR. PRASHANT S LOKHANDE

Made with ♥ on the Notion Press Platform

www.notionpress.com

To my family, parents, my wife Suchita and friends, whose unwavering support and encouragement have been my guiding light throughout this journey. Your love and belief in me have fueled my passion and perseverance. This book is dedicated to you, for being my constant source of inspiration and strength.

Contents

Preface

Welcome to "Mastering Cyber Hygiene: A Practical Guide for Individuals." In today's digitally interconnected world, where our personal and professional lives are increasingly reliant on technology, the importance of cybersecurity cannot be overstated. From safeguarding our sensitive information to protecting our digital identities, the need to prioritize cybersecurity has never been more critical.

This book is born out of a passion for demystifying cybersecurity and empowering individuals with the knowledge and tools needed to navigate the digital landscape safely. Drawing from my years of experience in industry, research, and academia, I've endeavored to create a comprehensive resource that caters to readers at all levels of technical proficiency.

In these pages, you'll find a wealth of practical advice, actionable strategies, and real-world examples aimed at helping you bolster your cyber defenses. Whether you're a cybersecurity enthusiast looking to deepen your understanding or a novice seeking guidance on basic security practices, this book is designed to meet you where you are and guide you towards a safer and more secure digital future.

I encourage you to approach this book with curiosity, an open mind, and a willingness to learn. By adopting a proactive approach to cybersecurity and implementing the practices outlined within these pages, you'll not only enhance your own digital resilience but also contribute to creating a more secure online environment for everyone.

Thank you for embarking on this journey with me. Together, let's master cyber hygiene and pave the way towards a safer digital world.

Dr. Prashant Lokhande

The Basics of Cybersecurity

This chapter will delve into the essential pillars of good cyber hygiene, providing actionable methods to enhance your digital defenses.

Definition of cyber hygiene and its significance

Cyber Hygiene: Cyber hygiene refers to the proactive steps that people take to ensure the security and privacy of their online activities and information. Taking care of your digital self is similar to caring for your physical health. Just like you brush your teeth and wash your hands to avoid pathogens, cyber hygiene routines help you avoid security dangers and protect your data.

Imagine your internet presence as a castle. The stronger the walls (passwords), the cleaner the moats (security software), and the more vigilant the guards (awareness), the less probable it is that your security will be compromised. Neglecting digital hygiene weakens your defenses, making you a vulnerable target for fraudsters.

Why Cyber Hygiene is More Important Than Ever?

Data breaches are commonplace. Every year, millions of people are victims of data breaches, which expose personal information such as passwords, bank details, and even medical records.

- *Cybercrime is on the rise*: Hackers are growing more clever, using advanced tactics to exploit loopholes. Cybercrime is projected to cost trillions of dollars yearly.
- *Our Lives Are Digital*: Almost everything is connected online, including employment, healthcare, entertainment, and banking. A hack can completely destroy your life.

Investing in excellent cyber hygiene protects not only your data but also your privacy, finances, and identity. It enables you to take charge of your online security and navigate the digital world with confidence.

1.1 The Main Pillars of Cyber Hygiene

- *Password Management*: Learn how to create strong, unique passwords and store them securely.
- *Software Security*: Make sure your operating systems, apps, and anti-virus software are up to date.
- *Phishing Awareness*: Learn how to recognize and avoid phishing scams that attempt to steal your information.
- *Safe Browsing Practices*: Be wary of the websites you browse and the links you click.
- *Social Media Privacy*: Change your privacy settings and be careful what you publish online.
- *Multi-Factor Authentication*: When possible, use multi-factor authentication to add an additional layer of protection.
- *Data Backup*: Back up your vital data on a regular basis to avoid accidental loss or ransomware assaults.

Introduction to common cyber threats individuals face

Individuals entrust a tremendous quantity of personal information to the digital sphere, including banking information, social media profiles, medical records, and financial paperwork. While interconnection improves our lives, it also exposes us to a variety of cyber risks.

Understanding these dangers is critical to protecting yourself and your data. This chapter will introduce you to the most prevalent cyber hazards that people experience, assist you in identifying potential risks, and provide you with the information you need to keep secure online.

1. Malware: The phrase "malware" refers to a variety of harmful software intended to harm your device or steal your data. The most common types of malware are:

- Viruses are self-replicating programs that can destroy your system and files.

- Worms are similar to viruses, but propagate more quickly across networks.
- Trojan horses are malicious programs that disguise themselves as genuine software in order to get access to your system.
- Ransomware encrypts your files and demands payment for decryption.
- Spyware steals sensitive information, such as passwords and surfing history.

2. Phishing: This social engineering method is designed to fool you into disclosing sensitive information. Phishing emails, texts, and phone calls frequently spoof legitimate sources such as banks, social networking sites, or even friends. They may include urgent demands or tempting offers that encourage you to click on dangerous websites or download infected documents.

3. Social Engineering: In addition to phishing, social engineering uses psychological manipulation to obtain access to your information or systems. This can include impersonation, fraudulent websites, emotional manipulation, and even physical trickery.

4. Weak Passwords: Think of your password as the lock on your digital door. Weak passwords, such as easily guessable terms or credentials that have been reused, are equivalent to leaving your door open for thieves.

5. Unsecured Wi-Fi: Public Wi-Fi networks are frequently unencrypted, making them simple targets for hackers to intercept your data. Avoid sensitive activities such as online banking while using public Wi-Fi, and consider utilizing a VPN for enhanced security.

6. Insecure Websites: Avoid websites with inadequate security protocols (HTTP instead of HTTPS) or suspicious URLs. These websites may be used to steal your data or install malware on your device.

7. Data Breaches: Unfortunately, data breaches are becoming more regular, exposing millions of people's personal information at once. Keep track of the companies with which you share your data, and update it on a regular basis.

8. Smishing and Vishing: Like phishing, these threats employ text messages (smishing) or phone calls (vishing) to deceive you into disclosing personal information or clicking on dangerous websites.

9. Physical Threats: Although less common, physical attacks like stolen gadgets or malware-infected USB drives can still compromise your data. Be aware of your physical surroundings and secure your electronics correctly.

10. Unpatched Software: Outdated software frequently has security flaws that attackers can exploit. To stay protected, make sure to update your operating systems, programs, and anti-virus software on a regular basis.

Remember that cyber threats are continuously developing. Staying educated and adopting excellent cyber hygiene can greatly lower your chances of becoming a victim.

Importance of personal responsibility in maintaining cybersecurity

In today's digital world, personal responsibility is critical to ensuring cybersecurity. As people rely more on digital technologies for communication, financial transactions, and other areas of daily life, a proactive and responsible approach to cybersecurity becomes critical. Here are some significant arguments that emphasize the need for personal responsibility in preserving cybersecurity:

1. Protection of Personal Information

Digital Footprint: People leave a large digital footprint through their online activity on social media, forums, online shopping, etc. Taking personal responsibility entails protecting personal information, such as usernames, passwords, and sensitive data, to avoid illegal access and misuse.

2. Prevention of Identity Theft

Fraud Protection: Personal responsibility is critical for preventing identity theft, a common cyber hazard. Responsible online behavior, such as recognizing phishing efforts and avoiding providing sensitive information, can help prevent identity theft and financial fraud.

3. Minimizing Cyber Risks

Identifying Threats: Being aware of frequent cyber hazards and actively educating oneself about potential risks are examples of personal responsibility. This knowledge enables people to notice and respond to risks quickly, lowering their chances of falling victim to cyber attacks.

4. Securing Financial Assets

Safe Online Transactions: Personal responsibility includes protecting the security of online financial transactions. Using secure payment methods, routinely reviewing bank accounts, and exercising caution when sharing financial information online all help to create a secure financial environment.

5. Preserving Digital Reputation

Being Cautious Online Behavior: Taking personal responsibility entails engaging in responsible and ethical online behavior. Avoiding cyberbullying, abstaining from publishing incorrect information, and having a positive internet presence all help to protect one's online reputation.

6. Contributing to Collective Security

National and Global Impact: Recognizing that individual acts have far-reaching consequences for collective security is critical. Individuals who take personal responsibility for cybersecurity help to create a safer digital environment for themselves and the community as a whole.

7. Implementing Cyber Hygiene Practices

Regular Maintenance Personal responsibility requires implementing and upholding proper cyber hygiene habits. This involves keeping software and systems up to date, using strong and unique passwords, and exercising caution while accessing internet information.

8. Education for Empowerment

Awareness Promotion: Individuals that prioritize personal responsibility in cybersecurity frequently contribute to community education and awareness-raising efforts. This empowerment extends to educating others about the importance of digital security measures.

9. To prevent system compromises, secure devices.

Personal responsibility includes securing personal gadgets, including cell phones, PCs, and IoT devices. Implementing security measures such as firewalls and antivirus software can help prevent data breaches.

10. Embracing a Proactive Mindset and Continuous Learning.

Personal responsibility in cybersecurity entails an ongoing commitment to continual learning. Individuals that stay updated about emerging threats, evolving technology, and best practices are better able to adapt to the ever-changing cyber scene.

In essence, personal responsibility is the foundation of a strong cybersecurity strategy. It enables individuals to actively participate in securing their digital lives, creating a safer and more resilient online environment for themselves and the larger digital community. Individuals can help strengthen the collective defense against cyber dangers by raising awareness, educating others, and taking proactive measures.

CHAPTER TWO

Anatomy of Cyber Attacks

Cyber attacks can take many different forms, each with its own set of methods and aims. Understanding the anatomy of these attacks is critical for individuals seeking to identify and successfully mitigate possible dangers. Here's a look at some frequent sorts of cyber attacks.

1. Phishing Attacks: Overview: Phishing attacks are fraudulent attempts to steal sensitive information, such as usernames, passwords, and financial details, by impersonating a trusted institution.

- Tactic: Attackers frequently employ false emails, bogus websites, or messages to fool people into providing sensitive information. Phishing attacks frequently use psychological manipulation and haste to boost their success rate.

2. Malware Infections: Overview: Malware, or malicious software, refers to dangerous programs that penetrate computer systems and steal sensitive information.

- Types: Malware can take the form of viruses, worms, trojans, ransomware, or spyware. Each type has unique traits and goals, which range from data theft to system interruption and financial extortion.

3. Social Engineering Exploits: Overview: Social engineering attacks use human psychology to trick people into disclosing sensitive information or compromising security.

- Here are several examples: Pretexting (creating a scenario to extract information), baiting (enticing victims with a reward), and tailgating (gaining physical access by following authorized persons) are all examples of social engineering tactics.

4. Ransomware Incidents: Ransomware is a sort of malware that encrypts a user's files or system, making them unavailable and demanding payment (typically in cryptocurrency) to decrypt them.

- Impact: Ransomware attacks may be severe, resulting in data loss, financial extortion, and operational disruptions for individuals and companies.

5. Overview: Man-in-the-Middle (MitM) attacks intercept communication between two parties to eavesdrop, manipulate, or spoof genuine communication.

- Methods: Attackers may attack network infrastructure weaknesses or employ tactics such as ARP spoofing or DNS hijacking to intercept data packets and modify the user-server connection.

6. Overview: Distributed Denial of Service (DDoS) attacks flood a target system or network with malicious traffic, making it inaccessible to legitimate users.

- Objectives: DDoS assaults interrupt services, resulting in downtime, financial losses, and reputational damage to enterprises and organizations.

7. Zero-Day Exploits: Zero-day exploits target previously undisclosed vulnerabilities in software or hardware that do not have a patch or fix available.

- Risk: Zero-day exploits pose substantial dangers because they allow attackers to start targeted assaults on individuals or organizations before security updates are created and released.

Understanding the anatomy of cyber assaults enables users to detect suspicious activity, develop proactive security measures, and respond effectively to prospective threats. Individuals can strengthen their resilience against hostile actors in the digital realm by being educated about evolving cyber threats and implementing a multi-layered cybersecurity strategy.

2.1 Real-world examples of cyber incidents and their consequences

Actual instances of cyberattacks and their fallout in India

i) Data Breaches

- Air India (2022): Due to a misconfigured server, over 4.9 million customers' personal information—including names, contact information, and passport details—was exposed online. People may have been vulnerable to financial fraud and identity theft as a result.
- BigBasket (2020): Hackers gained access to and disclosed approximately 20 million customers' personal data, including hashed passwords, phone numbers, email addresses, and names. The company suffered financial losses as well as reputational harm from this episode.
- Zebra (2021): The phone numbers, email addresses, and transaction details of more than 100 million Mobikwik members were compromised due to a data breach. This raised questions about user security and privacy on the platform.

ii) Ransomware Attacks Attacks

- AIIMS Delhi (2021): A ransomware attack affected the All India Institute of Medical Sciences Delhi, causing major disruptions and postponing patient care. This incident demonstrated how susceptible healthcare organizations are to cyberattacks.
- The Maharashtra State Electricity Distribution Company Limited (2020): experienced a disruption in power supply to millions of consumers due to a ransomware attack carried out by hackers. This incident illustrated the potential effects of cyberattacks on crucial infrastructure.
- Wipro, 2021: The IT services provider Wipro had a ransomware attack that reduced its productivity and resulted in losses of money. The necessity of strong cybersecurity procedures in big businesses was brought to light by this occurrence.

iii) Another Cyber Event

- Aadhaar Data Leak (2018): Unauthorized access to the Aadhaar database, which held millions of Indians' sensitive personal data, was allegedly possible. Concerns over data security and privacy in the government system were brought up by this.
- Social Media Disinformation Campaigns: Inciting violence, influencing elections, and undermining public confidence in institutions have all been accomplished through the dissemination of false information via social media platforms. This emphasizes how difficult it is to combat false information online in India.
- Mobile Banking Frauds: Phishing and malware attacks have made people believe they are sending money or giving private information, and this is a growing problem in India. This has reduced confidence in digital payment systems and resulted in financial losses.

Consequences of these incidents

- Financial losses: Data breaches, ransomware attacks, and other cyber incidents can cause individuals and organizations to suffer significant financial losses.
- Reputational damage: Cyber incidents can harm businesses and institutions' reputations, resulting in a decline in trust and customer loyalty. Privacy violations: Exposed personal information can result in identity theft, fraud, and other negative outcomes.
- Operational disruptions: Cyberattacks can cause major disruptions to vital infrastructure and services, resulting in financial losses and inconveniences.
- Psychological impact: Cybercrime victims may suffer stress, anxiety, and other emotional distress.

The aforementioned instances demonstrate the wide array of cyber risks that Indian individuals and enterprises must contend with. To reduce the dangers and repercussions of such incidents, it is critical to maintain awareness of cyber threats, implement robust cybersecurity procedures, and notify authorities of any suspicious activity.

2.2 Understanding the Motivations Behind Cyber Attacks

Cyberattacks have a wide range of intricate objectives, from political agendas to self-interest. Below is a summary of several important reasons:

- Revenue: Attackers most frequently use this motive in an attempt to steal money or important data. Among the strategies are:
- Ransomware: encrypting data and requesting ransom payments for its decryption. Data breaches: Taking financial or personal information for credit card fraud, identity theft, or selling on the black market. Cryptocurrency mining: Using compromised systems to mine cryptocurrency without the owner's knowledge.
- Spies: Confidential information can be stolen by nations, businesses, and people for a variety of reasons.
- Industrial espionage: stealing intellectual property or trade secrets to obtain a competitive edge. Military espionage: obtaining information about military plans and capabilities. Political espionage: snooping on activists or opponents of politics.
- Hacktivism: These assaults have political or ideological underpinnings and are frequently meant to create a stir or increase awareness:
- DDoS attacks: Sending a website with excessive traffic to the point of unavailability. Defacing websites: Modifying a website's content to convey a message.
- Disclosing private information: revealing details in an effort to bring a company into disrepute or shame.
- Private grudges: People may choose to target particular individuals or groups for retaliation, rage, or other reasons.

Additional Motives

- Challenge and recognition: The intellectual challenge of hacking or the desire for fame might serve as motivators for some attackers.
- Chaos and disruption: Certain attacks seek to sow division or create general disturbance without any particular objectives.

Knowing these reasons is essential for

- Creating successful cybersecurity strategies: Knowing the targets of attackers aids in the prioritization of defenses; Attributing attacks: Determining the motive can help reduce the number of potential suspects; Preventing future attacks: Gaining insight into attacker motivations can aid in the development of more potent deterrent and prevention strategies.

It's crucial to remember that: Attackers frequently have a variety of motivations; Motivations change with time; With advancements in technology, new incentives could appear. Through keeping up with the always changing danger landscape and comprehending the motivations behind cyberattacks, people and organizations can enhance their defenses against harm.

CHAPTER THREE

Password Management and Authentication

Having strong password management and authentication procedures is crucial in the linked world of today, where almost every element of our lives has a digital counterpart. The effectiveness of our authentication procedures and the strength of our passwords are crucial in guaranteeing cybersecurity, as they protect critical company data as well as personal information. Understanding the importance of strong password management and authentication procedures is crucial as we traverse the complexity of the digital landscape and build the foundation for a safe and resilient digital future.

3.1 Best practices for creating strong and unique passwords

The first line of defense in the always changing world of cyber dangers is having strong passwords. A strong password safeguards your online identity and valuable information, much like a strong lock does for your house. You will leave this class with the skills and know-how necessary to make memorable and impregnable passwords.

The Foundations of Strong Passwords

1. Length Is Important: Forget the minimum of eight characters. Try to use 12 characters or more, with each extra character adding to the intricacy. Recall that it takes ten times longer to crack a larger password.
2. Diversity Is Essential: Be unpredictable. Combine numbers, symbols, and upper-and lowercase letters to create something like "!@$%^&()_+-=[]{};':\",<.>/?|". Steer clear of personal information (birthdates, pet names) and keyboard patterns like Qwertyuiop.
3. Singularity is Crucial: Avoid the temptation to use the same password for several accounts. Every platform needs its own special guardian to

ensure that if one fails, it won't happen to others.

4. Passwords Instead of Words: Have memorable phrases instead of single words (dictionary fodder!), such as "PurpleMonkeysLoveTacos2023!" They are more complicated and lengthy without losing their memorable quality.
5. You should befriend password managers: Managing multiple distinct passwords can be very taxing. Think about utilizing a password manager, which is a safe haven that creates and maintains secure passwords for you.

Beyond the Fundamentals

- Activate two-factor authentication (2FA): This requires a second verification step, such as a code from your phone, even in the event that your password is hacked, adding an additional layer of security.
- Never divulge your passwords: Handle them with the same utmost discretion as your toothbrush!
- Be on the lookout for phishing attempts: Avoid opening attachments from senders you don't know or clicking dubious links. Perhaps they are attempting to obtain your password.
- Update your passwords frequently: Think about switching accounts every few months, especially for important ones like email and banking.

Keep in mind: Having strong passwords is crucial for maintaining good online hygiene. You may create a strong defense against online dangers and have a safer, more secure online experience by adhering to these recommended practices. So, strengthen your digital fortress and put your password-mastery to the test!

Try this: Use your imagination! To come up with passphrases that are memorable and distinctive, combine your interests, hobbies, and inside jokes. Enjoy yourself while doing it!

3.2 Introduction to password managers and their benefits

Managing countless passwords for multiple accounts in today's digital world can resemble navigating a wild password jungle. Making powerful and distinctive ones, let alone remembering them all, seems like an insurmountable task. But do not worry, password managers are here to help you regain control and security over your online life. Envision a safe deposit box containing all of your passwords, each distinctive, intricate, and nearly impenetrable. This is how password managers work their magic. They generate your passwords as well as store them, so you never have to worry about creating weak, simple passwords.

But why is using a password manager recommended? Here are a handful of the advantages:

- Unbreakable Security: Do away with the need to reuse passwords or depend on easy combinations. Every account has strong, random passwords generated by password managers, which make them nearly impossible to decipher.
- Effortless Convenience: Forget about fumbling with your login credentials. You can easily access all of your accounts with just one master password.
- Automated Logins: Put an end to time-consuming typing! Password managers let you save time and stress by automatically filling in your login details.
- Enhanced Security: To further prevent unwanted access, a lot of password managers come with two-factor authentication (2FA).
- Peace of Mind: You may unwind and enjoy your internet activities worry-free if you know your passwords are secure.

Are you curious? Fortunately, there are a plethora of free and paid password managers to choose from, each with unique features and advantages. Your unique requirements and tastes will determine which one is best for you.

Are you prepared to assume command of your online safety? With the help of a password manager, begin your road towards a password-free future and enjoy the freedom and peace of mind it offers!

Examples of Password Managers

Here's an inside look at a few appreciated free and paid solutions to assist you in selecting the ideal one for your requirements:

Free of Cost Password Managers

- Bitwarden: An open-source alternative with cross-platform compatibility, robust security features, and infinite password storage. Perfect for tech-savvy people who value control and openness.
- Dashlane: provides a free plan with limitless password storage along with standard features like safe sharing and automated login. Excellent for

people looking for a simple sharing option and an easy-to-use interface.

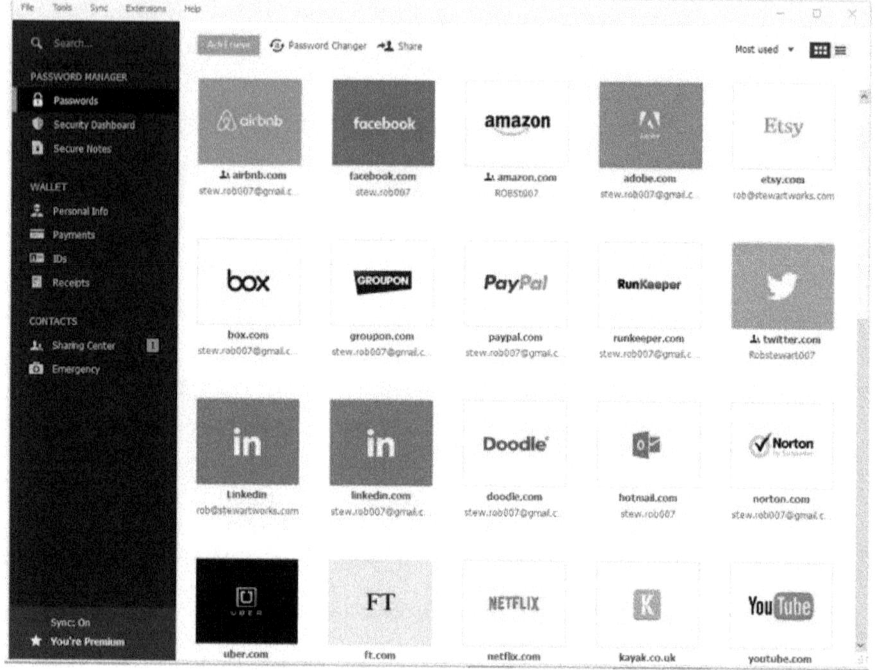

Fig. 3.1 Dashlane Password Manager

NordPass: includes a free subscription with limitless passwords, data breach monitoring, and multi-device syncing. Ideal for people who appreciate functionality and simplicity in security.

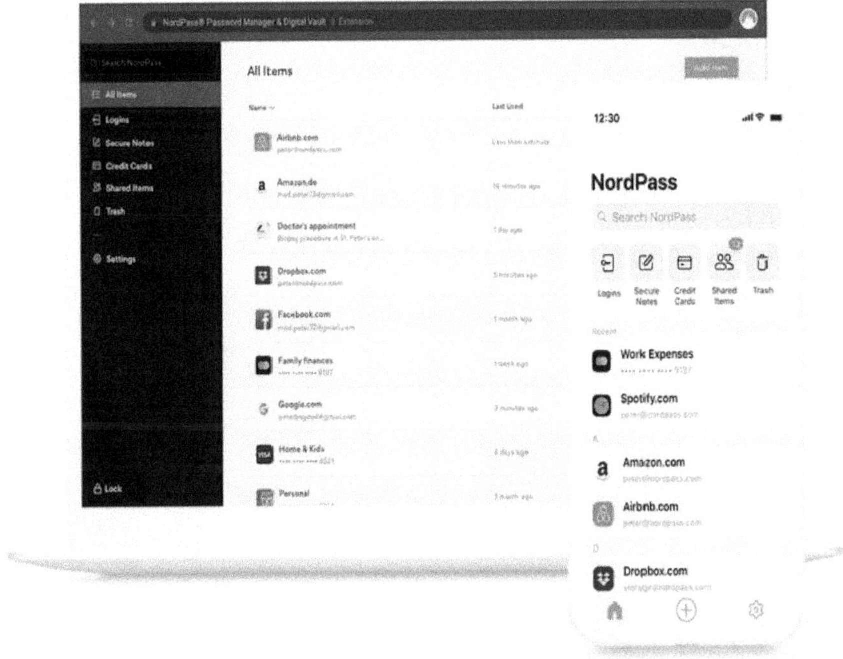

Fig. 3.2 NordPass Password Manager

Keeper: offers a mobile-friendly, password-protected, limited-time free plan. It is excellent for people who place a high priority on mobile security and portable basic password management.

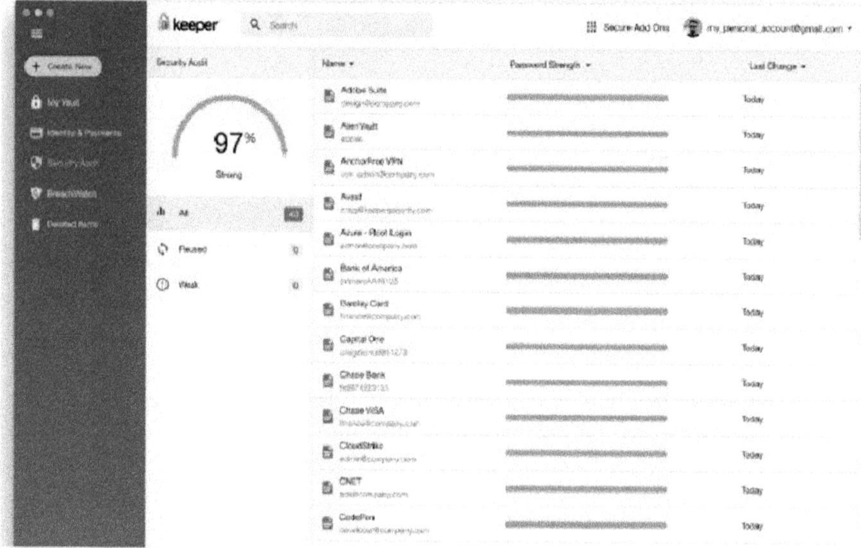

Fig. 3.3 Keeper Password Manager

LastPass Free: provides limitless password storage for one type of device (desktop or mobile) under a free plan. Ideal for individuals just beginning to manage their passwords on one device.

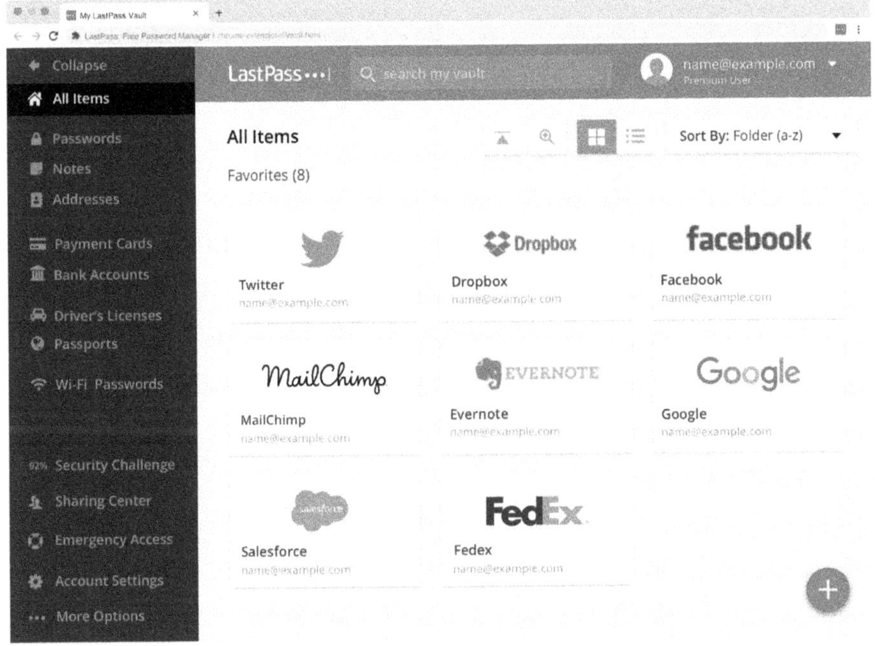

Fig. 3.4 Lastpass Password Manager

Premium Password Organizers

i) Password: Well-known for its strong security, user-friendly layout, and abundance of features, including travel mode and family plans. Perfect for people and families looking for cutting-edge features and complete safety.

ii) Dashlane Premium: Adds VPN access, password changes, and dark web monitoring to the base free subscription. Ideal for consumers seeking extra security features and comfort.

iii) NordPass Premium: Adds secure file storage, priority customer assistance, and data breach notifications to the free plan. Excellent for anyone looking for more features and robust security measures.

iv) RoboForm: Provides enhanced form filling, password inheritance, and cloud backup in its premium subscriptions. Perfect for heavy users that need sophisticated security features and extensive form management.

Keep in mind that the "best" password manager will ultimately rely on your personal requirements and preferences. When making your decision, take into account aspects like budget, device compatibility, security features, and convenience of use.

Bonus Advice: Examine the free trials provided by certain premium password managers to gain practical experience prior to making a commitment.

3.3 Importance of two-factor authentication (2FA) for enhanced security

The Power of Two-Factor Authentication (2FA) : Imagine having only a cheap lock to protect your house. It could keep away casual intruders, but a determined thief could still simply get through. Imagine now installing an alarm system and a deadbolt a far more formidable protection, don't you think? The significance of two-factor authentication (2FA) in the modern digital age is aptly demonstrated by this analogy.

What is 2FA?

Consider it an additional security measure on top of your password. Passwords are very important, but they can be taken by phishing scams, data breaches, or even just plain human mistake. Adding a second verification step to your password, 2FA makes it much more difficult for someone else to gain illegal access.

How does 2FA work?

The most popular techniques consist of:

- Time-based codes: Every few minutes, an exclusive code that you receive over text message, email, or app changes. To log in, you must enter this code in addition to your password.
- Hardware tokens: You enter codes generated by these physical devices when logging in.
- Biometric authentication: The second factor can be voice, facial, or fingerprint recognition technology.

What makes 2FA significant?

Here are some reasons to think about turning on 2FA for all of your significant accounts:

- Enhanced security: The extra verification element makes it extremely improbable that someone will get illegal access, even if your password is compromised.
- Defense against phishing: Scammers frequently attempt to fool you into disclosing your password. Even if you become a victim, the attacker won't have access to the second factor if you use 2FA.

- Peace of mind: Having additional protection for your accounts lowers the possibility of identity theft and financial loss while also enhancing your peace of mind.

Getting 2FA started

2FA is a feature that most online services and platforms offer. Usually, you can easily enable it in your account settings. Investigate your possibilities and select the approach that best fits your requirements and tastes without delay.

i) Instagram: Two-factor authentication safeguards your account by mandating the entry of a code whenever you attempt to log in from an unfamiliar device. Follow the steps given below for two-factor authentication to safeguard your Instagram account.

Turn on two-factor authentication

1. Click ☰ More in the bottom left, then click Settings ⬡.

2. Click **See more in Accounts Center**, then click **Password and security**.

3. Click **Two-factor authentication**, then select an account.

4. Choose the security method you want to add and follow the on-screen instructions.

Turn off two-factor authentication

1. Click ☰ More in the bottom left, then click **Settings** ⬡.

2. Click **See more in Accounts Center**, then click **Password and security**.

3. Click **Two-factor authentication**, then select an account.

4. Choose the security method you want to turn off and follow the on-screen instructions.

Fig. 3.5 Two-factor Authentication for Instagram. Source: Instagram

When you set up two-factor authentication on Instagram, you'll be asked to choose one of three security methods: You'll need to have at least one of these set up in order to use two-factor authentication.

- Authentication app: (recommended): Download an authentication app, such as Duo Mobile or Google Authenticator to get login codes. This security method is recommended, because you can add multiple devices connected to an account so they can all get login codes. Note: Two-factor authentication through an authentication app can only be turned on using the Instagram app for Android and iPhone.

- Text message: Instagram will send a login code to your mobile number.
- WhatsApp: Turn on the text message security method first. Then, you can turn on the WhatsApp security method to get login codes from WhatsApp.

ii) Facebook: If you set up two-factor authentication, you'll be asked to enter a special login code or confirm your login attempt each time someone tries accessing Facebook from a browser or mobile device that we don't recognise. You can also get alerts when someone tries logging in from a browser or mobile device that we don't recognise.

- Turn on or manage two-factor authentication
- Click on your profile picture in the top right, then click Settings and privacy.
- Click Settings.
- Click Accounts Centre, then click Password and security.
- Click Two-factor authentication, then click on the account that you'd like to update.
- Choose the security method that you want to add and follow the on-screen instructions.

When you set up two-factor authentication on Facebook, you'll be asked to choose one of three security methods:

- Tapping your security key on a compatible device.
- Login codes from a third-party authentication app.
- Text message (SMS) codes from your mobile phone.

Once you've turned on two-factor authentication, you can get ten recovery login codes to use when you're unable to use your phone.

iii) LinkedIn: Two-Step Verification is a great way to protect your account. Two methods of verification are available: text (SMS) verification, and authenticator app verification. LinkedIn recommends the authenticator app as the preferred two-step verification method. An authenticator mobile app gives you easy, secure access to online accounts you can use for a second layer of security in addition to your password entry. One example of an authenticator app is Microsoft Authenticator.

Follow the steps below to set up the authenticator app for Two-Step Verification:

- Install an authenticator app from your app store (such as Microsoft Authenticator).
- Select the profile icon at the top of your LinkedIn homepage and select Settings & Privacy.
- Under the Sign-in & security, select Two-step verification to enable or change your two-step verification method.
- Enable two-step verification and choose Authenticator App as your verification method. Select Continue and submit your LinkedIn password.
- Open your authenticator app and tap Add Account or click the + icon at the top right corner. If this is your first time setting up an account on the app, you'll be prompted to set up an account.
- Select Other and use "LinkedIn" as the account name.
- Enter the secret key provided by LinkedIn into the Authenticator App.
- Enter the 6-digit verification code generated by your authenticator app to verify your device.

Now your device is ready for two-step authentication. Whenever you log in from a new device, open your Authenticator app and enter the code when prompted for two-step verification.

Important: The authenticator app connection is unique to each mobile device and each app install. If you uninstall the app, reset your mobile phone, or get a new mobile phone, you will need to set up the authenticator app again.

iv) Gmail: With 2-Step Verification, also called two-factor authentication, you can add an extra layer of security to your account in case your password is stolen. After you set up 2-Step Verification, you can sign in to your account with:

- Your password
- Your phone

Process to initiate 2FA as follows

- Open your Google Account.
- In the navigation panel, select Security.
- Under "How you sign in to Google," select 2-Step Verification Get started.
- Follow the on-screen steps.

Keep in mind: 2FA is not flawless, although it greatly improves security, it's still important to use strong passwords and be on the lookout for unusual activity. You're being proactive about protecting your important data and your online identity by implementing 2FA. Raising your security level now will provide you the piece of mind that comes with knowing that an additional shield is in place to secure your accounts.

Convenience vs. security: While hardware tokens provide the highest level of security, they may not be as convenient as other approaches.

Teamwork is required: Inspire your loved ones to add two-factor authentication to their accounts.

CHAPTER FOUR

Device and Network Security

Our gadgets and networks act as entry points to a world of connection that encompasses everything from professional communication and entertainment to personal financial information and entertainment. Safeguarding these digital lifelines is now essential rather than optional. Let us introduce you to the world of device and network security, a complex barrier that protects our priceless information and virtual interactions. This chapter explores the fundamental levels of security, from strong firewalls to watchful antivirus software, enabling you to confidently traverse the digital terrain. By being aware of potential dangers and the resources at your disposal to counter them, you can turn your networks and devices from weak points into strongholds equipped to handle the constantly changing demands of the digital era.

4.1 Tips for securing computers, smartphones, and other devices

In the hyperconnected world of today, a vast quantity of sensitive and personal data is stored on our gadgets. Protecting these digital assets is crucial as they include money and medical records, as well as professional documentation and priceless memories. You will leave this session with useful advice on how to harden your gadgets, whether they are smart home appliances, capable laptops, or even convenient cellphones.

Constructing Robust Foundations

1. Authentication and Passwords

- Strong & Unique Passwords: Instead of using straightforward dictionary terms for every account, use complex, unique passwords. If you want safe and easy storage, think about using password managers.
- Activate 2FA: Whenever possible, use two-factor authentication (2FA) to add an additional degree of security. Even if your password is leaked, this still needs a second verification step, such as a code from your

phone.

2. Updates to Software

- Keep it Current: Pay attention to those update alerts! Updating your firmware, operating systems, and apps on a regular basis patches vulnerabilities and keeps your gadgets safe from the most recent attacks.
- Automatic Updates: For a stress-free method, think about turning on automatic updates.

3. Malware & Virus Protection

- Act as an Active Defender: To identify and get rid of harmful threats, arm your devices with trustworthy antivirus and anti-malware software. Decide on a trustworthy supplier and plan frequent scans.

4. Safety of Networks:

- Secure your Wi-Fi: Turn on encryption (WPA2 or WPA3) and use a strong password for your Wi-Fi network. Refrain from using unprotected public WiFi networks.
- Firewall Protection: To add an additional line of protection, filter incoming and outgoing network traffic using a firewall.

Special Advice for Devices
i) Computers

- Manager Access Limit: Limit administrator privileges to accounts that are actually in need of them in order to reduce the possible harm caused by vulnerabilities.
- Watch Out for Phishing: Watch out for shady attachments, websites, and emails. Never provide private information on untrusted websites.

ii) Mobile Devices

- App Permissions: Exercise caution when granting downloaded apps access. Grant entry solely to the essential features.

- Lost/Stolen Device Protection: To increase security in the event that your device is lost or stolen, turn on options like data erasing and remote tracking.

iii) Digital Home Appliances

- Update Default Passwords: Make sure you don't use the default passwords. Create secure, one-of-a-kind passwords for any device.
- Secure Networks: Disconnect your primary devices from your smart gadgets and connect them to another, secure network.

Keep in mind: Security is a continuous procedure rather than a one-time patch. Keep yourself updated on new risks, modify your procedures as necessary, and take advantage of a safer, more secure online environment!

Bonus Tip: To reduce possible losses in the event of device compromise, regularly backup your critical data to external drives or cloud storage services.

4.2 Guidelines for securing home Wi-Fi networks and routers

Protecting Your House Wi-Fi: In the connected world of today, our houses are digital hubs humming with online activity rather than merely physical places. Our Wi-Fi network is the cornerstone of this connectivity, so keeping it secure is crucial. With the knowledge and resources in this book, you'll be able to turn your house Wi-Fi into a secure fortress and safeguard your gadgets, information, and privacy.

Establishing a Robust Foundation

- Change the Default Password: For your Wi-Fi network, choose a strong, unique password instead of the manufacturer's easy-to-guess password. Employ a mix of numerals, symbols, and capital and lowercase letters.
- Activate WPA Encryption: Depending on your network, select WPA2 or WPA3 encryption. By blocking data, these protocols practically prevent unwanted users from accessing your network.
- When not in use, disable the guest network: If you provide a guest network, make sure it is disabled when not in use to avoid unwanted access.
- Hide Your Network Name (SSID): Although it's not 100% secure, concealing your SSID can help make it less noticeable to would-be attackers.

High-Tech Security Protocols

- Update the firmware on your router: To fix vulnerabilities and guarantee optimum performance, update the firmware on your router on a regular basis.
- Enable Firewall: Firewalls are typically integrated into routers. In order to further safeguard your network, enable them to screen both incoming and outgoing traffic.
- Make sure your device passwords are strong: Remember to create secure passwords for all of the gadgets linked to your Wi-Fi, including smart speakers, computers, and cellphones.
- Disable Remote Access: Turn off remote access to your router's settings unless you really need it. As a result, there is less chance of unwanted access from outside your network.
- Consider a VPN: Use a Virtual Private Network (VPN) for enhanced security and privacy, particularly when utilizing public Wi-Fi.

Further Advice

- Access Limit: Keep your Wi-Fi password private from other people. Give access only to devices and people you can trust.
- Exercise Caution When Using Public WiFi: Steer clear of using open Wi-Fi networks to access private information. For further security, utilize a VPN if required.
- Keep an eye on connected devices: The majority of routers include an interface for viewing the devices linked to your network. Keep an eye out for any unfamiliar gadgets and take necessary action.
- Remain Updated: To maintain a safe network, keep yourself informed about the most recent cybersecurity risks and best practices.

Keep in mind: Security is a continuous endeavor. You can give your family and devices a safe and secure home Wi-Fi environment and enjoy the digital world with peace of mind by putting these tips into practice and being watchful.

Importance of keeping software and firmware up to date

Remaining updated in the ever-changing world of digital media requires more than just knowing the newest memes and trends. It is essential to the function and safety of our devices and software, which are the very instruments we depend on. This course explores the benefits of updating firmware and software and will provide you with the information and drive to make necessary updates a priority.

The Power of Updates

- Security Patches: Critical security patches that address vulnerabilities exposed by hackers are frequently included in software and firmware updates. You may drastically lower your risk of malware infestations, data breaches, and other threats by remaining current.
- Improved Performance: Bugs and inefficiencies are frequently fixed via updates, which results in smoother performance, quicker load times, and an overall better user experience.
- New Features and Functionality: Upgrades might bring you fascinating new features and functionalities that broaden your digital horizons and improve the capabilities of your program.
- Compatibility: Updating your program keeps it compatible with more recent hardware and operating systems, averting future compatibility problems.

Developing an Update Routine

- Enable Automatic Updates: Try to enable automatic updates for your firmware, apps, and operating systems. By doing this, you may install updates automatically and avoid having to remember them by yourself.
- On a regular basis Look for Updates Here: Periodically check for updates, especially for critical software, even if automatic updates are enabled. Prioritize Critical Updates: Updates designated as critical or security updates should be installed right away since they fix significant vulnerabilities.
- Read Update Descriptions: Skimming through the update descriptions in brief can help you prioritize the most critical updates by providing you with an overview of what's being added or addressed.

Overcoming Reluctance to Update

- Apprehension of Disruption: Updates may occasionally result in brief disruptions. The advantages of enhanced functionality, performance, and security, however, greatly exceed these little drawbacks.

- Technical Issues: To learn more about an update's possible effects, check online or with technical support if you have any questions.

Remember: Updating firmware and software is crucial for keeping a safe and effective digital environment. You can prioritize updates, create a thoughtful update schedule, and keep up with the newest technological developments while protecting your devices and data.

Bonus Tip: To streamline the procedure and guarantee uniform protection, think about utilizing a patch management tool to automate the updating process across all of your devices.

CHAPTER FIVE

Safe Online Behaviour

These days, the internet is an important part of our lives. We give the digital world a lot of personal information and important interactions when we do everything from banking and shopping to following our passions and spending time with loved ones. However, with all the potential benefits that come with the internet world also come some risks, much like any large landscape. In this setting, the ability to engage in safe online behavior becomes increasingly important, enabling us to confidently navigate the digital jungle while reducing potential risks. This journey explores the fundamental procedures that serve as the cornerstone of online safety, giving you the information and resources you need to navigate the digital world responsibly, mindfully, and, in the end, with peace of mind. So grab a seat, and let's examine the fundamentals of responsible online conduct, which will turn you from a careless tourist into an informed and capable digital adventurer!

5.1 Strategies for recognizing and avoiding phishing scams

Phishing scams are a persistent concern in the digital age, where information is openly shared and online interactions are normal. These dishonest attempts to trick people into disclosing private information, such as credit card numbers, passwords, or personal information, can have disastrous results. But do not worry! You may greatly lower your chance of being a victim of these nefarious schemes by being aware of the techniques used by phishers and putting them into practice.

Spotting the Warning Signs

- Suspicious Sender: Be cautious when responding to texts, emails, or phone calls from senders you don't know or from people who seem to be from reputable companies but have odd phone numbers or email addresses.

- Phishing emails frequently instill a sense of urgency, pressuring you to take urgent action in response to a purported security breach, account issue, or time-limited offer. Reputable establishments hardly ever put pressure on you to respond right away.
- Spelling and Grammar Mistakes: Phishing attempts frequently use misspellings, grammar mistakes, or poor wording. Examine the wording very closely.
- Suspicious Attachments or Links: Even if an email appears to be from someone you don't know, avoid clicking on links or opening attachments. Before clicking, hover your cursor over the link to view the full URL.
- Requests for Personal Information: Requests for personal information via email or unsolicited calls are not often made by legitimate organizations. Requests for social security numbers, credit card information, or passwords should be avoided.

Defense Techniques

- Verify Sender Identity: To confirm the sender and the content of an email, get in touch with the organization directly via their official website or phone number if you have any doubts about its legitimacy.
- Never Click on Doubtful Links: Before clicking, hover your cursor over the link to view the full URL. Don't click if it appears suspicious or if the displayed text doesn't match.
- Make Use of Secure Passwords and Turn on 2FA: Your accounts are further secured by two-factor authentication (2FA) and strong, one-of-a-kind passwords.
- Be cautious While Using Public Wi-Fi: Refrain from accessing private data or creating accounts on unprotected Wi-Fi networks. A VPN might be used to increase security.
- Keep Software Updated: Phishers may take advantage of security holes in outdated software. Update your browsers, apps, and operating system on a regular basis.
- Educate Yourself: Keep up with the most recent phishing schemes and frauds. Resources and instructional materials are available from numerous security and government groups.

Keep in mind

Attempts at phishing are always changing. Be alert and modify your tactics as necessary.

Report a scam if you believe it to be one. This aids law enforcement in locating and neutralizing bad offenders. [Believe your instincts.] Something is probably off if it feels that way. Never be afraid to ask questions or confirm questionable messages twice.

You may greatly lower your chance of being a victim of phishing scams by implementing these tactics and staying watchful. You can also move around the digital world with more assurance and security. Recall that your best defenses against these dishonest strategies are knowledge and skepticism. Thus, have a safer online experience by remaining educated and exercising caution!

5.2 Tips for safe browsing and downloading content from the internet

Phishing scams are an everyday risk in the digital age, when information is widely shared and online interactions are typical. Devastating outcomes may result from these dishonest attempts to trick victims into disclosing private information such as credit card numbers, passwords, or personal information. Don't worry, though! You may greatly lower your chance of being a victim of these nefarious schemes by being aware of the techniques used by phishers and putting forward workable solutions.

Recognizing Warning Signs

- Unknown Sender: Be on the lookout for unseen emails, messages, or phone calls, as well as those posing as representatives of respectable companies but using strange email addresses or phone numbers.
- Pressure and Urgency: Phishing emails frequently instill pressure, telling you that you must act right away because of a purported security breach, account issue, or time-limited promotion. Reputable groups seldom coerce you into taking quick action.
- Phishing attempts frequently exhibit typographical flaws, grammatical errors, or odd language. Examine the phrase closely.
- Suspicious Attachments or Links: Even if they seem genuine, avoid opening attachments or clicking links in emails from senders you are not familiar with. To view the URL before clicking, hover your cursor over the link.
- Requests for Personal Information: It is uncommon for legitimate companies to make unwanted phone calls or email requests for personal information. Requests for passwords, credit card information, or social

security numbers should be avoided.

Defense Methodologies

- Confirm Sender Identity: To confirm the sender and the contents of an email, get in touch with the sender's organization directly via their official phone number or website.
- Avoid Clicking on Dubious Links: Verify the URL by hovering over the link before clicking. Avoid clicking on anything that doesn't seem right or doesn't match the text that is displayed.
- Set up 2FA and Use Robust Passwords: You can further secure your accounts by using two-factor authentication (2FA) and strong, one-of-a-kind passwords.
- Use Public Wi-Fi with Caution: Steer clear of sensitive data access and account logins on public Wi-Fi networks. To enhance security, think about utilizing a VPN.
- Maintain Up-to-Date Software: Phishers may take advantage of security holes in out-of-date software. Update your operating system, browsers, and apps on a regular basis.
- Educate Yourself : Remain up to date on the most recent phishing schemes and con artists. Educational materials and tools are available from numerous government departments and security groups.

Keep in mind

Phishing attempts are ever-changing. Be alert, and adjust your tactics as necessary.

Report any scams you believe to be fraudulent. This aids in the authorities' efforts to find and eliminate bad actors.

Rely on your instincts. It's probably something if it feels strange. Never be afraid to investigate and confirm any strange messages.

You may greatly lower your chance of falling for phishing scams by implementing these tactics and staying alert. This will allow you to traverse the digital world with more security and confidence. To combat these deceitful tactics, keep in mind that alertness and skepticism are your best weapons. So, have a safer online experience, exercise caution, and be aware!

5.3 Guidelines for interacting safely on social media platforms

Social media is a dynamic environment that entertains, informs, and connects us. Like any busy public area, it does, however, also present certain risks. In order to ensure a safe and enjoyable experience when using these platforms, let's examine some fundamental rules for responsible interaction and self-defense:

Take Care with What You Share

- Think Before You Post: Before clicking "share," think about the possible outcomes of your posts. Keep in mind that content is hard to fully remove once it's on the internet.
- Privacy Settings: To manage who can view your information and postings, become aware of and modify your privacy settings.
- Personal Information: Steer clear of disclosing private information such as your address, phone number, or bank account number. Location Sharing: Use caution when allowing location sharing, particularly when it's happening in real-time, since it may jeopardize your security and privacy.

Participate with Respect and Accountability

- Remember to Be Courteous and Kind: Real people are behind the screens. Even if you disagree with someone's viewpoints, still treat them with respect.
- Watch Out for Online Trolls: Avoid responding to criticism or hostility. Report inappropriate behavior and leave the conversation. Fact-Check Information: Exercise caution when disseminating rumors or unconfirmed information. Do your homework and double-check information before posting.
- Honor the rights of others: Remember copyright rules and refrain from spreading anything without authorization or due credit.

Guarding Yourself Against Fraud and Dangers

- Watch Out for Phishing: Take caution when clicking on dubious links, communications, or demands for personal data. Check the sender's identity and legitimacy before making any clicks.
- Strong Passwords: To increase security, use strong, one-of-a-kind passwords for all of your social media accounts. Beware of Fake Profiles: Be wary of profiles that appear too good to be true or make money-related requests. Seek out badges of authentication and keep an eye out

for any unusual activities.

- Report Any Questionable Behavior: Never be afraid to alert the platform's support staff about any questionable activities, communications, or profiles.

Further Advice

- Take Breaks: There is an overload of social media. Take regular pauses to prevent overexposure and detachment.
- Manage Your Time: To keep a healthy balance in your life, set boundaries on how much time you spend on social media.
- Avoid Making Comparisons: Idealized depictions of reality are common on social media. Put your own needs first and avoid comparing yourself to other people.
- Request Assistance: Ask for assistance from friends, family, or online support groups if you are the victim of cyberbullying, harassment, or any other harmful influence.

You can help make social media safer and more pleasurable for everyone by following these rules and encouraging an appropriate online persona. Recall that our interactions in the actual world are reflected in the digital realm. When you approach it with understanding, respect, and a good measure of caution, you'll be able to navigate the social waters with positivity and confidence!

i) How to Stay Safe on Instagram?

Instagram has put out a bunch of safety tools and resources to help us stay safe online. Here are the best ways to keep your Instagram account safe, both on and off the app.

To safely log in to Instagram, use two-factor security: With two-factor authentication, you need to know something (like your username and password) and have something (like your phone) in order to log into your Instagram account from a device you are not familiar with. This helps keep your account safe. This means that someone who knows your password but not your phone cannot get into your account.

Two-factor authentication protects your account by demanding a code if you attempt to log in using a device we don't recognize. Steps to enable two-factor authentication is explain in chapter 3.

i) Be careful about who can see your posts : Every Instagram account can be seen by everyone in the community by default. You can decide who sees your information by making your account private. One more thing you can do with a private account is get rid of friends without blocking them. To make your account secret, do the following: Press the "On" button next to "Private Account" on your personal page's "Settings" menu. When someone asks to follow you again, you will have to accept it.

ii) Don't let people see your posts by blocking them: With the blocking tool, you can still decide who can find and follow you on Instagram, even if your account isn't secret. To block an account, go to its profile, click the "..." menu in the top right corner, and then tap "Block User." The account owner will not be told that they have been blocked. The person will still be able to mention your Instagram username, but it will not show up in your Activity. Once you stop someone, they won't be able to talk about you again unless they know your new username.

iii) Pick and choose which comments to see: Most of the talk on Instagram happens in the comments. Instagram recently added the ability to filter comments based on keywords you choose or keywords Instagram chooses for you. If you see a comment on your post that you don't want, swipe left and tap the trash can to get rid of it. To stop people from leaving comments on a post, go to "Advanced Settings" and turn "Turn Off Commenting" to "On" before you post. Want to stop people from commenting on an old post? If you post something and then tap the "..." menu, you can change the state of comments on any post at any time.

iv) Pick a strong password : Mix at least six numbers, letters, and special characters (like! and &) into your password to make it hard to figure out. Don't post or give out your password to anyone you don't trust, not even a third-party app. If you use someone else's computer or phone, make sure you log out of Instagram and don't check the "Remember Me" box! For extra safety, set a lock code on your phone so that if you lose it, no one else can get into your account.

v) Tell someone about any abuse, bullying, threats, or fake identity: If you see something that seems fishy or a post that you think breaks the rules, tell Instagram about it! How to do it:

- Swipe to the left and tap the arrow to report a comment.
- Tap the "..." button and then "Report" to report a post or an account.
- You can also fill out a web form and send it to the Instagram review team.

vi) Help a friend who is in trouble :If you see someone writing about suicide or hurting themselves and think something needs to be done right away, call the police station in your area right away. You can report inappropriate material in the app by tapping the "..." menu next to any post and selecting "It's inappropriate." If there isn't an immediate threat of physical harm, do so. Choose the "Self-Injury" choice. You can call, text, or meet up with your friend to see how they're doing.

ii) How to Stay Safe on Facebook?

Staying safe on Facebook involves adopting similar principles to those outlined for Instagram, as both platforms are owned by the same company. Here are guidelines to help you stay safe on Facebook:

If you want to stay safe on Facebook, try following these rules:

1. Make sure your passwords are strong: Make sure your Facebook password is strong and unique. To make it safer, mix letters, numbers, and special symbols. Don't use information that is easy to figure out, like dates or everyday words.

2. Enable Two-Factor Authentication (2FA): Enable two-factor authentication for extra protection. Most of the time, this means getting a code on your phone, which you need to enter along with your password when you log in.

3. Change your privacy settings: Check and change your privacy settings often. You can decide who can see your personal information, posts, and friend requests. These settings can be changed to fit your tastes and level of comfort.

4. Be picky about the friends you make: Only accept friend requests from people you know and trust. Be careful when adding strangers because it can put your personal information at risk of being seen by people who might want to harm you.

5. Use the Blocking Feature: If someone is acting in a way that you don't like or that bothers you, you can use the blocking feature to stop that person from connecting with you on the platform. The person you blocked won't know about this move because it is private.

6. Be careful of phishing scams: Watch out for texts or friend requests that seem fishy. Don't click on links from people you don't know, and don't give personal information to accounts you don't know. Facebook will not text you and ask for your password.

7. Keep Software and Apps Up to Date: Make sure that your device's operating system is always up to date and that you regularly update your

Facebook app. Security fixes that help protect against holes are often included in updates.

8. Look over the permissions for third-party apps: When giving third-party apps access, be careful. You should only allow apps from sources you know and trust, and you should read the rights they ask for before letting them into your Facebook account.

9. Learn About Scams: Stay up to date on the most popular scams on social media. Be careful about giving out financial information, and make sure that offers or requests are real before you reply.

10. Report Doubtful Activities: Tell Facebook about fake profiles, spam, or other things that don't seem right. Reporting helps the site keep the environment safe by taking the right steps.

11. Review Your Account behavior Regularly: Look over your account history and behavior from time to time. If you see any gadgets or places that don't look familiar, change your password and turn on two-factor authentication.

12. Learn about Facebook's safety features: Learn how to use the safety tools that Facebook offers. Keep up with any new settings or tools that can make your account safer.

Just by following these tips, you can make your Facebook account much safer and lower your chances of running into online threats.

CHAPTER SIX

Data Protection Best Practices

In today's digital world, protecting our critical data is no longer a luxury, but rather a need. Protecting sensitive information necessitates a proactive approach and adherence to best standards, whether it be personal data or private company records. Understanding and putting into practice efficient data protection procedures is essential, regardless of whether you're a business managing enormous volumes of consumer data or an individual worried about internet privacy. This chapter explores the crucial best practices you should implement to guarantee that your data is safe, compliant, and able to withstand ever changing threats. Prepare to go out on a task to build a stronghold for data protection!

6.1 Overview of data privacy laws and regulations

What is data privacy?: Data privacy is the protection of people's individual information and their right to decide how companies and other entities gather, utilize, distribute, and store it. It includes making sure that people can reasonably expect their personal information to be kept private and safe, and that organizations handle this information responsibly and in line with the laws and rules that apply.

Every day, huge amounts of personal data are gathered, stored, and processed. It is very important to know the laws that protect data privacy. The overview of the most important data privacy laws and rules are given as follows, which will help you find your way through this complicated web of rules.

The World Scene: Data privacy laws are very different around the world. Some places already have set frameworks for privacy protection, while others are still working on them. These people are important:

1) The General Data Protection Regulation (GDPR) in the EU is generally seen as the gold standard for data privacy. It gives people a lot of rights over their personal data, such as the ability to access, correct, and delete it.

2) California: The California Consumer Privacy Act (CCPA) and the California Privacy Rights Act (CPRA) give Californians the same data rights as the GDPR, plus they make businesses more open about how they gather and use data.

3) Brazil: The Lei Geral de Protecão de Dados (LGPD) is a lot like the GDPR. It stresses openness, personal control, and responsibility for those who are in charge of data.

4) In India: A new law called the Digital Personal Data Protection Act (DPDPA) protects all kinds of personal data in India. It focuses on reducing the amount of data that is stored, keeping it local, and sending it across borders.

The main ideas are: Different laws have different standards, but most of them are based on these basic ideas:

- Transparency and Notice: People have the right to know what information is being taken, how it is being used, and who it is being shared with.
- Consent: Before collecting and using someone's info, organizations must get their clear permission.
- Data Security: Businesses must use the right security means to keep personal information safe from people who aren't supposed to see it, share it, change it, or delete it.
- Data minimization: Businesses should only gather and use the bare minimum of data needed for the tasks they've set out to do.
- Individual Rights: People usually have the right to see, change, or delete their personal information. They can also say no to processing it in some cases.
- Data leak Notification: When there is a data leak, companies are often required to tell people and the government.

Challenges with Compliance: It can be hard to follow data privacy rules, especially for businesses that do business in more than one jurisdiction. Here are some important problems:

- Keeping Up with Change: Laws about data privacy are always changing, so businesses need to keep up and change how they do things.
- Cross-Border Data Transfers: The rules for sending data across countries can be complicated and need careful thought and attention to detail.
- Data Mapping and Inventory: Finding and managing all of an organization's personal data can be a big job.

Guidelines: For an individual

- Learn about your rights under data privacy laws.
- Read privacy notices and policies to find out how your data is taken and used.
- Use your data rights: You have the right to access, change, or delete your data as needed.

Guidelines: For businesses

- Do a data privacy audit to find out how you collect and process personal data.
- Put in place the right security measures to keep personal data safe from people who shouldn't have access to it.
- Create clear privacy policies and procedures to make data practices clear.
- Get legal advice to make sure you're following all data privacy laws.

In conclusion: Data privacy is a complicated problem with rules that are always changing. People and businesses can better manage their data and find their way through the confusing rules about data privacy if they understand the basic ideas behind them and stay up to date on the laws that apply. Remember that your info is important, and that everyone needs to help protect it.

Extra Resources for reading

- The International Association of Privacy Professionals (IAPP) website can be found at https://iapp.org/.This link (https://iapp.org/)
- General Data Protection Regulation (GDPR) from the European Commission: https://commission.europa.eu/law/law-topic/data-protection_en("Data Protection") (https://commission.europa.eu/law/law-topic/data-protection")

- The California Privacy Rights Act (CPRA) can be found at [https://oag.ca.gov/privacy/ccpa].
- Digital Personal Data Protection Act 2023, India (https://www.meity.gov.in/writereaddata/files/ Digital%20Personal%20Data%20Protection%20Act%202023.pdf)

6.2 Strategies for protecting personal information online and offline

Protecting privacy has become very important in today's connected world, where personal data is constantly being shared and stored online. People need to take complete steps to keep their private information safe from identity theft, illegal access, and other privacy threats, whether they are online or off.

Tips for surfing Online

1. Make your passwords strong and unique: The best way to keep your internet accounts safe from people who shouldn't have access is to use strong, unique passwords. Use a mix of letters, numbers, and symbols, and don't use things like dates or names that are easy for people to figure out.

2. Two-Factor Authentication (2FA) should be turned on: Using two-factor authentication (2FA) makes things safer by needing a second way to prove who you are, like a code sent to your phone. This makes your online accounts much safer by making it harder for people who aren't supposed to be there to get in.

3. Update your software and apps often: It is very important for your protection to keep your operating system, software, and apps up to date. Updates often include fixes for known security holes, which makes it less likely that hackers will take advantage of them.

4. Be Careful When Sharing Personal Information: Be careful when sharing personal information online. You shouldn't share too much on social media sites, and you should check the privacy settings to see who can see your stuff.

5. Find and use Virtual Private Networks (VPNs): You might want to use a VPN when you connect to the internet, especially on public Wi-Fi networks. Hackers will have a harder time getting to your info if your VPN encrypts your internet connection.

6. Check your financial statements often: Pay close attention to your financial records to find any strange activity. If you notice any mistakes or unauthorized activities, you should tell your bank right away so that the damage is limited.

7. Attitude Awareness: Carefully look over apps before you download them. See if they have the right permissions and read reviews to find out how they gather and use your information. You should only install apps from sites you know and trust.

8. Protect Physical Documents: Keep important physical documents with personal information safe, like passports, social security cards, and bank records. You might want to use a safe or lockbox.

9. Get rid of sensitive papers: To stop identity theft, shred papers with personal information on them before throwing them away. This includes credit card offers, bank bills, and any other papers that have private information on them.

10. Don't share too much information: Be careful about giving out personal details in person. When filling out forms or polls, don't give information that isn't needed, and think about whether you really need to share some information.

11. Watch out for phone and email scams: Be careful if you get calls or emails from people you didn't ask for asking for personal information. Companies that are honest will not ask for private information over the phone or email. Make sure you know who is asking for information before you give it to them.

12. Make sure your wallet and devices are safe: Don't lose your cash, phone, or other electronic items. Lock your devices with passwords or PINs, and pay attention to your surroundings to avoid actual theft.

13. Keep an eye on your credit reports: Check your credit report often to see if there have been any strange or unauthorized actions. Reporting mistakes quickly can help keep your credit score from going down in the long run.

14. Be aware of shoulder surfing: When you use a public computer to enter a PIN or password, be aware of your surroundings. For extra safety, put your hand over the keyboard.

In conclusion: In a time when personal information is more easily stolen, it's important to think about privacy in a broad sense. People can make a strong defense against possible threats to their personal information by using both online and offline tactics. This makes both the online and offline worlds safer and more secure. Keep an eye out for new threats, learn about them, and use these techniques to protect your privacy in a world that is always changing.

6.3 Importance of data encryption and secure communication channels

It's impossible to overstate how important data encryption and safe communication routes are in this digital age where people are always sending and receiving private data. Businesses, people, and governments are relying more and more on digital platforms. To protect data accuracy, confidentiality, and authenticity, strong measures are needed more than ever. This piece talks about how important it is to encrypt data and use secure communication channels to protect digital assets and make sure that online interactions can be trusted.

Encrypting data is an important way to protect privacy and security.

1. The protection of privacy: Making sure that personal information stays private is one of the main reasons why data encryption is used. Encryption keeps data safe from people who shouldn't have access to it by using complicated algorithms to change it into a format that can't be read. This lowers the risk of data breaches and unauthorized releases.

2. Keeping personal information safe: Encryption is especially important for keeping private data like banking data, login information, and private messages safe. If there is a security breach, protected data is still useless to people who aren't supposed to see it, which limits the damage that could be done.

3. Being in line with data protection rules: Several laws around the world, including the GDPR, HIPAA, and CCPA, require the use of encryption to keep private and important data safe. Following these rules not only keeps businesses out of trouble with the law, but it also builds trust among users.

4. Ensuring the integrity of data: Data is kept safe from people who shouldn't be able to see it by encrypting it. Any changes or tampering with protected data leads to a completely different decryption output. This lets users know about possible security holes and keeps information reliable.

Building trust in digital interactions through secure communication channels

1. Secure Sockets Layer (SSL) and Transport Layer Security (TLS): The TLS and SSL protocols are very important for making sure that internet contact is safe. These cryptographic protocols protect private information sent between users and websites by encrypting data while it's in transit. They are used by web browsers.

2. VPNs, or virtual private networks: VPNs make links over public networks that are encrypted and safe. This protects the privacy of data

sent between devices. VPNs keep private information safe from people who might be listening in on networks that aren't secure. This is especially important for people who work from home.

3. Finally, there is End-to-End Encryption (E2EE): E2EE is a strong method used to protect conversations and file transfers in messaging apps and other communication systems. This method keeps data secured from the sender's device to the receiver's device, making it less likely that it will be intercepted.

4. Secure File Transfer Protocols: Safe file transfer protocols, like SFTP (Secure File Transfer Protocol) and SCP (Secure Copy Protocol), make sure that files are sent over networks safely. These protocols are very important for keeping private papers safe and stopping people from getting to them without permission while they're being sent.

In conclusion: As the digital world changes and cyber threats stay the same, data encryption and safe contact channels become more and more important for keeping digital assets safe. Strong encryption not only keeps private data safe from people who shouldn't have access to it, but it also builds trust among users and stakeholders. As people and companies learn how to use the internet, making data security a priority through encryption and safe communication channels is not only necessary, but also a key part of having reliable and strong online interactions.

CHAPTER SEVEN

Securing Online Transactions

Online purchases have become a normal part of our lives in this age of technology where ease of use is key. It's impossible to deny how easy it is to click and swipe when doing everything from buying groceries to handling bank accounts. However, every time we click, there is a chance that our personal and banking data could be stolen. No longer a nice-to-have, protecting online activities is a must. This piece talks about the most important things that people and businesses can do to feel safe shopping online and keep their financial information safe. Get ready to learn about the best ways to do business online safely and the latest technologies that make it possible. You do not have to worry about your safety and can enjoy the simplicity.

7.1 Safe practices for online shopping, banking, and financial transactions

These days, in this digital world, ease of use often comes with risk. Online platforms make it easier than ever to get goods, services, and banking tools, but they also leave people open to attacks. This chapter gives you the information and tools you need to stay safe in the digital world and keep your personal information and hard-earned money safe.

Smart Shopper

- Fortress of Security: Make sure any online shop you go to has a secure connection before you go in. If you see a padlock icon and "https" in the address bar, it means that the data is being sent securely.
- Brand Recognition: Only buy from stores with a good reputation and a history of doing business. Check out customer reviews and independent ratings of shops you're not familiar with before making a purchase.
- "Deal or Fraud?" Be careful with deals that look too good to be true. People fall for scams by offering deals that are too good to be true. Find

out what the average price is and compare deals from different places.

- Payment Skills: Credit cards are safer against fraud than debit cards. You might want to use a separate credit card for online purchases so that it's easier to cancel if your account is stolen. Check out safe ways to pay, like Apple Pay or PayPal.
- Looking over the receipt: Always look over order confirmations and receipts to make sure they are correct and look for any possible mistakes. Keep track of your deals so you can look back on them and settle any disagreements.

Bastion for Banking

- Password Powerhouse: Use a mix of capital and lowercase letters, numbers, and symbols to make strong, unique passwords for each bank account. Do not use private information like pet names or dates.
- Two-Factor Fortress: Use two-factor authentication (2FA) whenever you can. This makes things safer by needing a second verification code in addition to your password.
- Statement Scrutiny: Look over your bank accounts often to see if there is anything fishy going on. Tell your bank right away about any deals that you didn't make.
- Public Wi-Fi Danger: Don't do any financial transactions on public Wi-Fi networks because they can be spied on. Instead, connect to your home network or a safe mobile hotspot.
- Phishing Phantoms: Be wary of emails, calls, or texts that you didn't ask for that say they are from your bank. On these sites, you should never give out personal or banking information. Make sure that any communication you get straight from your bank is real.

Financial Strength

- Strong Software Shield: Always use the most recent versions of your operating system, antivirus software, and web browsers to fix security holes.
- App Armor: Only get apps from official app stores, and before installing them, check the developer's name. Don't give apps access they don't need.

- Social Secrecy: Be careful about what you post online, especially on social networks. Thieves can use personal information about you to target you with phishing scams or to steal your identity.
- Shredding Secrets: Before throwing away financial documents with private information, shred them to keep others from seeing them. Staying Informed: Keep up with the newest scams and threats to your internet safety. Sign up for trustworthy security blogs or emails to get timely tips and warnings.

Remember that you are responsible for your own safety online. When you follow these safe habits, you can feel good about using technology and keep your money and personal details safe.

Bonus Tip: If you want to make and remember strong, unique passwords for all of your online accounts, you might want to use a password organizer.

7.2 Recognizing and avoiding online scams and fraudulent websites

It is critical to identify and avoid online frauds and fraudulent websites in the current digital age, particularly in India, where the internet market is expanding rapidly. The subsequent strategies are crucial for recognizing and avoiding these online threats:

Identifying Online Frauds

1. Suspicious URLs and Domain Names: Examine URLs for misspellings or unusual domain extensions. A legitimate website may conclude with the extension '.com', whereas a fraudulent one may employ an atypical extension like '.co'. It is especially important to verify a secure connection (https://) before entering sensitive information or conducting transactions.

2. Highly Appealing offers: Be cautious of offers and deals that appear to be too excellent to be true. Scammers frequently entice their targets by promising substantial discounts or quick cash.

3. Unsolicited Communications: Exercise prudence when confronted with unsolicited emails, messages, or phone calls that request financial or personal information. It is advisable to authenticate the source prior to replying to any such communications.

4. Urgent Requests for Personal Information: It is uncommon for reputable organizations to request sensitive information through email or SMS.

Approach urgent inquiries for personal or financial information with skepticism.

5. Poor Website Design and Grammar Professional organizations make investments in meticulously crafted websites. Poor spelling, grammatical errors, and images of low quality are frequent indicators of a fraudulent website.

Countering the Use of Deceptive Websites

1. It is advisable to rely on reputable websites when engaging in online purchasing or utilizing services. Confirm the physical address and contact details of the organization. Verify ratings and evaluations left by previous customers.

2. It is advisable to employ secure and traceable payment methods, such as payment gateways (e.g., Paytm, Gpay, UPI etc.) or credit cards, rather than conducting currency transactions or direct bank transfers.

3. Examine Official Security Seals: - Search for security certifications from reputable organizations such as VeriSign, McAfee Secure, Norton Secured, and SSL certificates.

4. Enable Two-Factor Authentication (2FA): To enhance the security of your accounts, particularly when conducting financial transactions, enable 2FA.

5. Continually educate yourself regarding prevalent fraudulent schemes. As part of the Digital India initiative of the Indian government, Cyber Swachhta Kendra (https://www.csk.gov.in/) and similar websites offer cybersecurity-related information and resources.

6. It is recommended to use anti-virus and anti-phishing tools, including dependable antivirus software that should be installed and routinely updated, as well as browser extensions designed to detect and obstruct phishing websites.

7. Scam Reporting: - Inform relevant authorities, such as the National Cyber

Crime Reporting Portal (www.cybercrime.gov.in) or the Indian Computer Emergency Response Team (CERT-In), of any suspicious websites or schemes.

Common Online Frauds in India

1. Scams In the Form of Job Offers: Scammers present illegitimate employment prospects and demand advance payment for processing or training expenses.

2. Lottery and Prize Scams: - Injunctions requiring payment of a claim fee are communicated to victims who are duped into believing they have won a substantial sum of money or a prize.

3. Tech Support Scams: Scammers impersonate tech support agents in order to deceive their victims into divulging sensitive information about their computers or obligated to pay for superfluous services.

4. E-commerce Frauds: - On e-commerce platforms, fraudulent vendors offer products that do not exist or are substantially different from what was advertised.

By exercising caution and adhering to these recommendations, one can enhance their safeguarding against online frauds and fraudulent websites within the jurisdiction of India. It is of the utmost importance to prioritize online safety at all times and to exercise caution when confronted with any indicators of fraudulent behavior.

7.3 Tips for protecting payment card information and personal financial data

In this digital age, it is especially important to safeguard your payment card information and personal financial data, particularly in a market expanding at a rapid rate like India. Outlined below are several exhaustive suggestions to assist you in protecting your financial data:

Safeguarding Payment Card Data

1. It is advisable to visit secure websites prior to submitting any payment information. "https://" and a padlock icon should be present in the address

bar. Use private Wi-Fi networks when conducting online transactions. Use a private and secure Internet connection.

2. Enable Two-Factor Authentication (two-FA): Activate 2FA for all your online banking and financial accounts. This adds an extra layer of security by requiring a second form of verification, such as an OTP (One-Time Password) sent to your mobile phone.

3. It is advisable to consistently check one's bank and credit card statements for indications of unauthorized transactions. Urgently notify your bank of any suspicious activity that you observe. Raise the dispute by submitting dispute form to your bank.

4. Employ virtual debit and credit cards: Virtual cards are offered by some institutions for online transactions. Linked to your account, these are transient card numbers that provide an additional layer of security.

5. Establish Transaction Alerts: Activate email and SMS notifications for every transaction. This enables you to detect unauthorized activity immediately.

6. Use Trusted Payment Gateways: Utilize reputable and trusted payment gateways, such as UPI, Paytm, or Razorpay, when conducting online transactions.

7. Be Aware of Phishing Scams: - When receiving unsolicited emails or communications, refrain from downloading attachments or clicking on links. Conduct a correspondent verification prior to disclosing any personal information.

8. It is advisable to safeguard one's devices by installing and consistently updating antivirus and anti-malware software.
Utilize robust, distinct passwords for your online accounts, and modify them consistently.

Protecting Personal Financial Information: Suggestions

1. Prevent the Disclosure of Personal Information: It is advisable to refrain

from divulging personal financial information via email or phone, particularly when the request is unsolicited. In general, financial institutions and banks do not request sensitive information in this manner.

2. Employ Robust Passwords and PINs: Establish intricate passwords comprising a blend of numeric digits, capital letters, and special characters. It is not advisable to employ PINs that consist of easily guessed information, such as birthdays or sequential numbers.

3. Enable Account Lock Features: - If feasible, activate account lock features that secure your account automatically following a specified duration of inactivity or multiple unsuccessful login attempts.

4. It is advisable to refrain from storing card information online, specifically on e-commerce websites or online services. Each time, enter your payment information manually.

5. It is advisable to destroy financial documents that comprise sensitive information, such as credit card invoices, bank statements, and other similar items, prior to their proper disposal.

6. It is recommended to utilize digital wallets such as PhonePe, Google Pay, or Paytm when conducting transactions. Frequently, these devices offer an additional level of security by preventing merchants from accessing your card information.

7. It is advisable to consistently update software, including operating systems, browsers, and applications, to ensure they have the most recent security upgrades and updates.

8. Acquire Knowledge Regarding Scams: - Remain informed regarding prevalent schemes and fraudulent methods. One's initial line of defense against fraudsters is awareness.

Responding to and Reporting Fraud

1. Immediate Report of Lost or Stolen Cards: Immediately notify your bank if your card is lost or stolen so that unauthorized transactions can be

prevented.

2. In the event that any unauthorized transactions are detected, promptly communicate with your bank in order to dispute the charges and ensure the security of your account.

3. File a Complaint with Appropriate Authorities: - Utilize the National Cyber Crime Reporting Portal or the Indian Computer Emergency Response Team (CERT-In) to report cybercrimes.

You can substantially reduce the likelihood that your payment card information and personal financial data will be compromised by adhering to these guidelines. In the digital realm, safeguard your financial well-being by remaining vigilant and proactive.

CHAPTER EIGHT

Recognizing and Responding to Cyber Threats

8.1 Signs of a Potential Cyber Attack or Security Breach

Recognizing the warning signals of a potential cyber attack or security breach is critical for businesses and individuals to reduce risks and respond efficiently. Here are some frequent indications to look out for:

1. Unusual Network Activity : Sudden spikes or irregular patterns in network traffic may indicate illegal access or data exfiltration.

2. Unexpected System Outages or Performance Issues : Frequent system or program failures, slowdowns, or unexplained issues may indicate malware or a cyber attack.

3. Unexplained Changes in System Settings or Configuration : Unauthorized changes to system settings, configurations, or file permissions may indicate a security vulnerability.

4. Anomalies in Log Files : Examining log files for odd activity, such as several failed login attempts, access from strange IP addresses, or unauthorized changes, might aid in detecting potential security concerns.

5. Suspicious Emails or Phishing Attempts : Unexpected emails that request sensitive information, have suspicious attachments or links, or appear to be from unknown sources could be phishing attempts or malware delivery mechanisms.

6. Unrecognized Devices or Accounts : Unauthorized network connections or unfamiliar user accounts with enhanced rights may indicate a security breach.

7. Abnormal Access Patterns : Monitoring for unusual access patterns, such as accessing sensitive data at odd times or from strange locations, can aid in the detection of insider threats or compromised accounts.

8. Data Breach Notifications from Third Parties : Warnings from vendors, partners, or customers about unauthorized access to sensitive information may indicate a security breach.

9. Security notifications from Monitoring Systems : Automated security monitoring or intrusion detection/prevention systems may send out notifications for suspicious activity or known attack signatures.

10. Unexpected Financial Transactions or Account Activities : Unexplained financial transactions, unauthorized fund transfers, or fraudulent account activity could indicate a security breach or account compromise.

11. Missing or Altered Data : Data files or records that are missing, corrupted, or changed without reason may suggest unauthorized access or data tampering.

12. Unexplained System Privilege Escalation : Instances in which user accounts obtain unauthorized access to elevated privileges or administrative rights could indicate a security breach.

13. Security Tool Anomalies : Malfunctioning or deactivated security tools, antivirus alarms, or intrusion prevention systems could indicate an attempt to circumvent security measures.

14. Reports of Suspicious Activities from Users or Employees : Users or employees should report any suspicious emails, strange system behavior, or unauthorized access as soon as possible.

15. Abnormal Behavior Detected by User Behavior Analytics (UBA) Systems : UBA systems can identify deviations from normal user behavior, such as unusual login times or access to unfamiliar sites.

Organizations and people can better protect themselves against cyber threats by keeping aware and responding quickly to any signals of a potential cyber assault or security breach. Furthermore, implementing a comprehensive incident response plan is critical for effectively responding to and limiting the impact of security issues.

8.2 Immediate steps to take when confronted with a cyber incident

When confronted with a cyber event, taking early action is critical to minimizing damage and reducing future threats. Here is a guidance for what you should do:

1. Assess the Situation : Quickly determine the nature and severity of the situation. Determine whether it is an ongoing attack, a system failure, a data breach, or another form of cyber disaster.

2. Activate Incident Response Plan : If your organization has an incident response plan in place, activate it right away. This plan should define the measures to be taken in the event of a cyber incident, as well as the roles and duties of all staff involved.

3. Isolate impacted Systems : To prevent the attack or harm from spreading further, disconnect impacted systems or networks from the internet and other networked devices.

4. Preserve Evidence : Keep any evidence linked to the incident for forensic study and possible legal action. Do not tamper with or alter any data or systems that could jeopardize the inquiry.

5. Notify Relevant Stakeholders : Inform senior management, IT personnel, legal counsel, and any other parties affected by the occurrence. Communication should be clear and timely so that all parties are informed of the issue.

6. Contain the situation : Take action to limit the situation and prevent future damage. This could include establishing temporary security measures, restoring backups, or distributing fixes to vulnerable systems.

7. Engage External Support : If necessary, bring in external cybersecurity specialists, law enforcement agencies, or incident response teams to help with the investigation and resolution of the problem.

8. Implement Remediation Measures : After the incident has been contained, take remediation steps to fix any vulnerabilities or flaws that may have contributed to the incident. This could involve software updates, security patches, or modifications to security rules and processes.

9. Communicate with Stakeholders : Keep stakeholders updated on the status of the incident response efforts, including any updates on the investigation, remedial actions, and measures to prevent repeat events.

10. Perform a Post-issue study : Once the issue has been addressed, undertake a detailed post-incident study to identify lessons learned, areas for improvement, and recommendations for improving cybersecurity defenses and incident response capabilities.

Following these quick actions allows firms to efficiently respond to cyber attacks while minimizing the damage on their operations, reputation, and overall security posture.

8.3 Guidelines for reporting cyber incidents to relevant authorities or organizations

The Indian government has formed the Indian Computer Emergency Response Team (CERT-IN or ICERT) within the Ministry of Electronics and

Information Technology. Its principal job is to combat cyber security risks such as hacking and phishing, with the ultimate goal of improving overall internet security in India. On April 28, 2022, CERT-In issued instructions under section 70B(6) of the Information Technology Act of 2000, which addressed information security measures, protocols, prevention strategies, incident response plans, and cyber incident reporting, all of which aim to create a safer and more trustworthy online environment.

- All service providers, intermediaries, data centers, government entities, and corporate bodies must report cyber events within 6 hours of their occurrence or discovery, as defined in Annexure I to CERT-In.
- Incidents can be reported to CERT-In via email (incidents@cert-in.org.in), phone (1800-11-4949), or fax (1800-11-6969). The techniques and formats for reporting such incidents are available on the CERT-In website (www.cert-in.org.in), which will be updated as necessary.
- The "Citizen Financial Cyber Fraud Reporting and Management System" was created to connect 85 banks, payment intermediaries, and wallets to the Cybercrime Backend Portal. This allows citizens to report cyber financial fraud to National Helpline number 1930 or register online at Website: www.cybercrime.gov.in . The national helpline number is operational in all states and union territories.

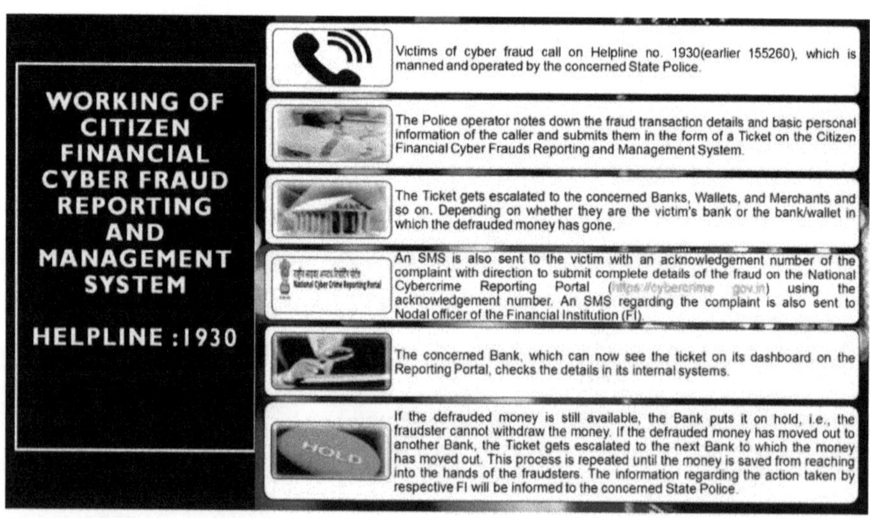

Fig. 8.1 Steps in cyber fraud reporting.

Mandatory Reporting: Certain types of cyber incidents, such as data breaches, cyber attacks, or security breaches involving sensitive personal information, may require mandatory reporting under Indian laws and regulations, such as the Information Technology (Reasonable Security Practices and Procedures and Sensitive Personal Data or Information) Rules, 2011.

Report to Law Enforcement: In cases involving illegal activity or major cyber risks, organizations should notify law enforcement agencies, such as Cyber Crime Cells or Cyber Police Stations, which have been formed in various Indian states and union territories.

Incident Reporting protocols: Organizations should develop internal incident reporting protocols to guarantee that cyber occurrences are immediately reported to the proper authorities and stakeholders. This may entail appointing certain persons or teams in charge of incident reporting and response.

CHAPTER NINE

Disaster Recovery and Backup

Disaster recovery and backup plans are like a safety net in the world of cybersecurity. They are necessary to keep businesses running and protect them from online threats. This chapter goes into detail about how regular data backups can help lessen the effects of cyber events.

9.1: Why are regular data backups important ?

Cyber incidents, such as data breaches and ransomware strikes, are now a constant danger in the digital world. Such events can have terrible effects, including losing data, having to stop working, losing money, and hurting your image. With these threats in the wings, it's clear how important it is to make regular backups of your data.

Keeping data from getting lost : Data includes important business information, user records, intellectual property, and operational data. It is the lifeblood of modern businesses. When there is a cyber incident, losing data can be very bad because it can slow down day-to-day operations and stop a company from growing. Regular backups of data act as a safety net, letting businesses quickly recover lost or damaged data. Businesses can keep their backups up to date to reduce the amount of data they lose and speed up the repair process. This cuts down on downtime and financial losses.

Making sure business keeps going : Business stability depends on being able to quickly get back to normal after something goes wrong. Without good backups, businesses risk long periods of downtime, which can have many negative effects, such as losing money, becoming less productive, and making customers unhappy. Regular data backups are very important for keeping a business going because they make it easy to quickly restore data and fix systems. Having strong backup plans is important for organizations because they help them get back up and running quickly after a disaster, hacking, or system error. This protects their operations and keeps stakeholders' trust.

How to Fight Ransomware Threats?: Ransomware attacks are very dangerous for businesses of all kinds because they encrypt important data and demand large ransom payments. When these kinds of threats happen, backups are a strong defense because they let companies avoid paying ransoms and recover data on their own. By keeping separate backups that are not connected to the internet, businesses can protect themselves from ransomware threats and stop the thieves from taking their data hostage. Also, regular backups make it much less appealing for hackers to target businesses because they can't make as much money off of encrypted data.

Keeping your reputation honest : In this highly linked world, reputation is very important, and one cyber incident can ruin a company's image forever. Long-term downtime and data breaches can hurt customers' trust, make stakeholders dislike the business, and hurt its reputation for a long time. Regular data backups are a key part of reducing these risks and ensuring that businesses can quickly recover from cyberattacks and keep their working integrity. By showing that they can handle problems, companies can improve their reputation and gain the trust of customers, partners, and investors.

Final Thoughts : Data backups that are done on a regular basis are the most important part of emergency recovery plans. They are like a lifeline in the crazy world of cybersecurity. By putting data resilience first and using strong backup methods, businesses can protect themselves from online threats, lessen the effects of disruptions, and ensure their long-term success. You can't say enough about how important regular backups are in this digitally risky era—it's not just a good idea, it's a business must.

9.2 Tips for Making Good Plans to Back Up Your Personal Data and Digital Assets

Personal information and digital goods are very valuable in a world that is becoming more and more digital. It is very important to keep these digital treasures safe, from loved photos and movies to important papers and financial records. This chapter shows you how to make a strong backup plan that will keep your personal information safe at all times.

Getting to Know Your Data

Identify Critical Assets: To start, make a list of all of your important digital assets. This includes important personal papers like passports and certificates, financial records like bank statements and tax returns, irreplaceable media like photos, videos, and music, and any other data you need to live your life.

Data Classification: Sort your data into groups based on how sensitive it is and how easy it is to replace. Important data that can't be replaced, like family photos, needs a stricter backup plan than music that is easy to download.

The 3-2-1 backup rule: The 3-2-1 backup rule is one of the most important parts of keeping your files safe. It tells you to keep three copies of your info, two on different types of media and one somewhere else. This redundancy makes sure that data is always available, even if hardware fails or there is a disaster.

- Three Copies: Having multiple copies protects against losing data because of a broken or faulty storage device.
- Two Media Types: Keep backups on different types of media (like a hard drive and the cloud) to protect against problems that only happen with certain kinds of media.
- One copy off-site: Keep at least one copy of your data in a place that is physically different from where you store your main copy. This protects against tragedies that happen in small areas, like fires or floods.

Strategies for implementing backups

- Backup Software: To handle the backup process, use backup software that is easy for everyone to use. Set up regular backups to keep your info in sync all the time.
- Cloud Storage: Use cloud storage services for an easy way to back up your files that is not located on your computer. A lot of cloud storage services have free plans that have plenty of room for photos and important documents.
- On-Site Storage: For local backups, use solid-state drives (SSDs) or portable hard drives. Rotate these files often to keep an up-to-date copy off-site.

Additional Things to Think About

- Encryption: Before putting private information in the cloud or on a flash drive, encrypt it. If your info gets lost or stolen, encryption keeps people from getting to it without your permission.

- Version control: If you need to go back to an earlier version of important data like papers, you might want to use version control tools to keep track of changes.
- Testing and Recovery: Make sure your backups work by testing them regularly and practice recovery situations to get used to the process.

In conclusion: By using these tips, you can make a full backup plan that will protect your personal information in case something unexpected happens. Remember that losing data can be very bad; a good backup plan will give you peace of mind and make sure you can always get back your digital treasures.

9.3 Introduction to data recovery tools and services

A Look at Some Data Recovery Services and Tools : Even if you have the best backup plans, you can still lose data if you delete something by accident, your hardware breaks, malware attacks happen, or something else unexpected happens. This chapter talks about data recovery services and tools that can get back data that has been lost or isn't available.

Learning How to Recover Data: Data recovery tries to get back data that has been lost, damaged, or isn't available from hard drives, solid-state drives (SSDs), memory cards, and even phones. How well data recovery works depends on how much data was lost and how good the recording media is.

Different kinds of data recovery tools: i) Free Data Recovery Software ii) Paid Data Recovery Software iii) "Do It Yourself" Data Recovery Kits

i) Free Data Recovery Software: You can find a number of free data recovery tools on the internet. In a simple way, they can get back files that you recently deleted. They may not be able to handle complicated data loss situations, though, because their features are often limited.

Free, open-source software for recovering lost data:

- **TestDisk and PhotoRec** (Windows, Mac, and Linux) work well together to get back lost files and sectors. Needs some technical know-how to use. To find the page where you can download TestDisk PhotoRec, search for it.
- **GNU ddrescue (Windows, Mac, Linux):** This program is designed to get data back from storage devices that aren't working. Mostly for advanced users. Look for "GNU ddrescue" to get to the page where you can download it.

- **Foremost (Windows, Mac, Linux):** Can be used for data recovery and data forensics to get back certain types of files, like pictures or papers, from damaged media. Look for "Foremost forensics" to find the page where you can download it.

Keep in mind that these are just a few examples. There are a lot more free and open-source data recovery tools out there. Before picking the one that best fits your needs, you should do some research and compare the features. Here is a list of some free data recovery tools and links to their websites:
Free Software to Get Back Lost Data:

- To get the original download page from Piriform for Recuva for Windows, search for "[Recuva Piriform]" (without the brackets).
- Disk Drill (Windows & Mac): To find their website, search for "[Disk Drill data recovery]" (without the quotes).
- To find the EaseUS Data Recovery Wizard Free download page, type "[EaseUS Data Recovery Wizard Free]" into a search engine without the quotes.

Remember that when you're looking for software to download, you should give priority to results from the official maker websites to avoid getting malware.

- TestDisk : - TestDisk's website can be found at https://www.cgsecurity.org/wiki/TestDisk.
- PhotoRec: - PhotoRec website can be found at (https://www.cgsecurity.org/wiki/PhotoRec)

These links should take you to the websites where you can get the program and learn more about how to use it and what features it has.

Note of importance: Even though free data recovery software can be useful, it may not have as many functions, recover as much data, or have a higher success rate than paid software. If you lose important data, you might want to look into professional data recovery services.

ii) Paid Data Recovery Software : Paid data recovery software has more features, such as the ability to restore raw data, support for more data types, and deeper scans.

- Stellar Data Recovery (Windows & Mac): Has a number of paid plans for different types of data loss. Search for "Stellar Data Recovery" on Google to find their page.
- R-Studio (Windows, Mac, Linux): With paid licenses, it offers professional-level data recovery tools. Search for their website by typing "R-Studio data recovery" into a search engine.
- GetDataBack (Windows): This program is known for being able to recover lost data in complex ways, and you can buy a license to use it. Find with "GetDataBack software" to go to their page.
- DM Disk Editor and Data Recovery (Windows): Has paid plans for full disk editing and data recovery. Searching for "DM Disk Editor" on Google to find their page.
- MiniTool Partition Wizard (Windows): Offers paid data recovery features along with tools for managing partitions. Search for "MiniTool Partition Wizard" on Google to find their page.

How to Choose the Best Paid Software?

- Look into features and capabilities: Compare the types of data and features that each piece of software can handle to find the best fit for your needs.
- Pricing and plans: Paid data recovery software usually has different pricing plans with different sets of functions. Check out their different pricing choices to pick the best one for you.
- Ratings and reviews from users: Find reviews and scores from other users that you can trust to get an idea of how well the software works and how easy it is to use.

Remember that paid data recovery tools might not be able to get all of your data back. Always put together a strong backup plan first.

iii) "Do It Yourself" Data Recovery Kits: DIY data recovery kits come with the tools and software that tech-savvy users need to try to recover their own data. But if you don't use these kits right, you could damage your info even more.

Here are some do-it-yourself data recovery tools and the links to their websites:

- R-Studio: http://www.r-studio.com/ is the website for [R-Studio].

- Do It Yourself DataRecovery iRecover : Website: (https://www.diydatarecovery.nl/)
- "DMDE" (DM Disk Editor and Data Recovery.): Website (https://dmde.com/) .
- Disk Drill : - http://www.cleverfiles.com/ is the website for [Disk Drill].
- Data Rescue : (https://www.prosofteng.com/data-recovery-software/) is the website.

These links should take you to the websites where you can learn more about the do-it-yourself data recovery tools, what they can do, and how to use them correctly.

Professional Services for Data Recovery: Professional data recovery services are the best way to get back lost data, especially when the situation is complicated. Companies that recover lost data use special tools, methods, and cleanrooms to make it more likely that the data can be recovered. These services can be pricey, though.

Choosing the Best Way to Do Things: There are a few things that affect your choice between data recovery tools and services:

- Severity of Data Loss: Free data recovery software might be enough for files that were just deleted. But if you lose important or complicated info, you might need to use a professional service.
- Technical Knowledge : If you know a lot about computers, you might want to use paid data recovery tools. But if you've lost a lot of data or aren't very good with computers, it might be safer to use a skilled data recovery service.
- Cost: The cheapest choice is to use a free data recovery tool. Professional services, on the other hand, cost a lot.

Important Things to Think About Before Data Recovery:

- Stop Using the Device: Stop using the storage device where you think data is being lost right away. More use can erase lost info, making it harder to get back.
- Talk to a professional: If the lost data is important or you're not sure what caused it, you should get an initial assessment from a professional data recovery service.

- Backing up data: No matter what data recovery method you choose, make backing up your restored data a top priority to avoid losing it again.

In conclusion: If you lose your info, data recovery tools and services can save the day. Learning about the choices you have and what they can't do will help you pick the best way to get back your important digital files. As the first line of defense against losing data, you should always make sure you have a strong backup plan.

CHAPTER TEN

Continuous Learning and Adaptation

10.1 Importance of staying informed about the latest cybersecurity threats and trends

The world of safety is always changing. Every day, new threats appear, old ones change, and new weaknesses are found. In this ever-changing world, it's important for both people and businesses to keep up with the latest cybersecurity threats and trends.

Why Should You Stay Informed?

Here are some strong reasons why it's important to stay up to date on hacking threats:

- Proactive Defense: Knowing things gives you power. If you know about the newest threats and how they work, you can protect yourself and your info before they happen. This means putting in place the right security measures, fixing bugs, and being wary of emails or links that seem sketchy.

- How to Stay Ahead of Attackers: Cybercriminals are always making their methods better. By following the newest trends, you can guess how they will change their strategies and take steps to stop them before they take advantage of new weaknesses.

- Making Smart Choices: For businesses, staying aware gives them the power to make smart choices about where to invest in security. Businesses can organize their resources and use them effectively to reduce the most pressing risks when they know what the most common threats are.

- Improved Detection and Response: Being aware of current threats makes it easier to spot possible security problems. Companies that know about the newest ways to attack can act quickly to stop breaches and limit the damage they cause.

- Maintaining Compliance: Many laws and industry standards require businesses to take the right safety steps. By keeping up with new threats, you can make sure you follow the rules and avoid possible fines for not doing so.

Strategies and Resources for Staying Informed

- Security News Websites and Magazines: Subscribe to security news websites, blogs, and magazines that are trusted by people in the security field. These sites keep you up to date on the newest threats, security holes, and best practices for keeping your information safe.
- Alerts and warnings about security: Sign up to get security alerts and tips from the government, software companies, and trustworthy security groups. These alerts let you know right away about newly found security holes and how to fix them.
- Security Webinars and Conferences: Go to cybersecurity workshops and webinars to learn from experts in the field. These events are great ways to learn about new threats and how to protect yourself from them.
- Training and Certifications for Security: Spend money on ongoing security training and licenses for you and your staff. People get the information and skills they need to spot and stop cyber threats through this training.

Final Thoughts : Because cybersecurity is always changing, keeping up to date is not a nice-to-have; it's a must. Keeping up with the latest dangers and trends will help you make smart choices, put in place strong security measures, and keep yourself and your important data safe from cyberattacks that are always changing. An attitude of "continuous learning" encourages proactive defense and adaptation, which helps you stay ahead of possible threats and keep your security strong.

10.2 Resources for ongoing cybersecurity education and training

Being alert all the time and wanting to learn are important in the fight against hacking. This chapter talks about useful tools for ongoing training and education in cybersecurity that will help you stay ahead of the changing threats.

i) **Free Online resources**

Online classes: There are many sites that offer free classes on cybersecurity. Some reliable sources are:

- **Coursera:** Offers a large selection of cybersecurity classes from top universities and industry leaders, with many of them being free to sign up for.
- **edX:** Offers free basic and advanced cybersecurity training, and some of them have certificate tracks that you can follow when you're done.
- **SANS:** The SANS Institute InfoSec Reading Room is a free library with a lot of white papers, security research reports, and vulnerability alerts.
- **OWASP:** The Open Web Application Security Project (OWASP) gives away free materials on the best ways to keep web applications safe, such as tip sheets, project guides, and online classes.
- **NIST:** The National Institute of Standards and Technology (NIST) Cybersecurity Framework is a free, voluntary framework that tells you how to find cyberattacks, protect yourself from them, react to them, and get back to normal after they happen.
- **CISA:** The Cybersecurity and Infrastructure Security Agency (CISA) helps people and businesses stay safe online by providing tools and advice.
- **Webinars and podcasts:** Sign up to receive security videos and webinars from experts in the field. A lot of them are free and give useful information about current risks and how to protect yourself.

ii) Resources that cost money

- Training and certifications for the job: Get professional training and certifications in cybersecurity, such as Certified Ethical Hacker (CEH) or Security+, to improve your skills and job chances. These schools give in-depth training on certain areas of security and can lead to credentials that are recognized in the field.
- Training for specific vendors: A lot of the time, companies that sell software and security solutions offer training programs that are specific to their goods and services. People who want to get the most out of the security features in the tools they already have may find these apps useful.

iii) Extra Resources

- Security Community Forums: Join online security communities and forums to meet other security experts, share your knowledge, and learn about new threats.
- Books and articles: Read books and articles about hacking written by experts in the field on a regular basis. These sites give in-depth looks at current threats and the best ways to defend yourself.

Choosing the Right Tools

- Identify Your Needs: Think about what you know now and what your security goals are. Are you looking for general information or do you want to become an expert in a certain subject?
- Think About How You Learn: Do you learn best through reading, watching videos, taking online classes, or doing hands-on labs?
- Dedication to Time: Think about how much time each item will take. Pick the choices that work best for your schedule and how fast you learn.

In conclusion: Individuals and businesses need to keep learning about and practicing cybersecurity in order to stay safe as risks change. By using the many free and paid tools out there, you can keep learning new things, get better at things you already know how to do, and help make the internet a safer place. Never forget that cybersecurity is an ongoing process. If you want to stay ahead of cyber threats and protect your data and yourself, you should accept lifelong learning.

10.3 Strategies for maintaining vigilance and adapting to evolving cyber threats

When it comes to cybersecurity, things are always changing, so people and businesses need to be proactive to stay alert and respond to new threats. Cybercriminals are always changing their methods and strategies, so it's important to always be one step ahead. This chapter talks about different ways to be more alert and successfully adapt to new cyber threats.

Figuring Out the Threat Environment: Before putting cyber threat defense plans into action, it's important to have a full picture of the current threat scenario. This means keeping an eye on industry trends, threat data feeds, and platforms for sharing information all the time. By keeping up with new dangers, businesses can better plan for possible risks and weaknesses.

Regular reviews of risks : It is important for organizations to do regular risk assessments to find weak spots in their systems. To do this, the security of systems, networks, and apps must be checked to find any possible holes. Organizations can prioritize security steps and use their resources well if they know how much risk they are exposed to.

Putting Defense-in-Depth into Action : Defense-in-depth is a multi-layered method to cybersecurity that means putting in place many layers of security controls to protect against different types of attacks. Among these are firewalls, intruder detection systems, endpoint security solutions, encryption, and controls on who can access what. By using a variety of defenses, businesses can lessen the damage that online threats do and make it less likely that they will be successful.

Constant Watching and Responding to Incidents :Companies can find and fix security problems right away when they keep an eye on their networks and systems all the time. Security information and event management (SIEM) systems are used for this. These systems gather and analyze data from different sources to find strange behavior and possible security holes. Also, organizations can contain, lessen, and recover from cyberattacks more effectively when they have a clear incident reaction plan.

Employee Awareness and Training :Human error is still one of the main reasons for security breaches, so making sure employees are aware of the risks and training them are important parts of any cybersecurity plan. Employees can better spot and handle possible threats if they get regular training on security best practices, phishing awareness, and incident response processes. Creating a culture of security knowledge also gets people to take responsibility for their cybersecurity duties.

Working together and sharing information : Cybersecurity is a group effort that needs businesses, government bodies, and industry partners to work together and share information. Organizations can learn a lot about new threats and weaknesses by joining threat intelligence sharing groups and industry-specific information sharing and analysis centers (ISACs). Stakeholders can improve their overall safety and resilience by sharing information and best practices.

Putting money into new technologies : Because cyber dangers are always changing, companies that invest in new technologies can get better at finding and stopping threats. Artificial intelligence, machine learning, and behavioral analytics are some of the new technologies that can help find and stop online threats in real time. Companies can improve their ability to find and respond to new cyber threats by using these tools.

Final Thoughts : Staying alert and changing with changing cyber threats is a constant task that needs a proactive, multifaceted approach. Organizations can improve their cybersecurity and reduce the risks that cyber threats offer by learning about the threat landscape, doing regular risk assessments, putting defense-in-depth into action, and encouraging a culture of security awareness. To stay ahead of the constantly changing threat environment, people must also work together, share information, and invest in new technologies. In a world that is becoming more connected, these strategies can help businesses better protect their assets, data, and image.

www.ingramcontent.com/pod-product-compliance
Lightning Source LLC
Chambersburg PA
CBHW040129150726
48005CB00015B/2428